What Are The Odds?

A Collection of Astounding Stories

Robin Wood

Catherine!
Tell [illegible]!
[signature: Robin Wood]

Robin Wood Ministries
Edmond, Oklahoma

Published by Robin Wood Ministries
1729 W 33rd, Suite B
Edmond, OK 73013
(602) 690-5303
rjwood@cox.net

Printed in the United States of America

Table of Contents

Thanks Is Not Enough

The word "Thanks" is just not enough to tell the following people how much they mean to me. This book would not have been possible without my family. So many of these "What are the Odds" stories would just not have happened if not for Carma, Leah, Brady and Annie. You have shared my life and experiences at the highest level. Together, we have celebrated a "What are the Odds" life. Thanks for every part you play in my life.

Thanks to all the people in these unique stories. You have been the major actors and actresses in God's unfolding drama in your personal lives.

But the publishing of this book would not have happened without the following. I want to extend my warmest gratitude to Wilma for the countless hours of editing the original manuscripts. I am an oral communicator and you are the reason these stories are in written form. Huge thanks to Patsy Snyder, my assistant. Without you Patsy, this project would never have been completed. I don't know how to thank you for the countless hours of editing, typing, encouraging, and saying, "We are almost there!" You are an incredible daughter and friend in the Lord. You are totally off, off, off the chart! Huge thanks to Tim McCormick who I believe made a "What are the Odds" phone call out of nowhere to reach me. Tim and I had not talked for over a couple of years, and when he called I knew he was my key to finding a graphic designer. When I returned that magical phone call, I was directed to Gina Sample. Tim simply said, "Gina is one of the best layout designers I know." He also said, "She probably won't do your book, because she has to love the material to accept the project." Thanks for the vote of confidence. So what are the odds Gina accepted to design the layout for these stories? Gina you are awesome and brilliant. To top off the project, I want to thank Keith Hojnacki for the exceptionally creative cover design. Keith, you always go beyond my wildest imagination. Words can't express my gratitude for all you have done for CMA over the past three years. You are the best graphic designer I have ever been associated with. Finally, how can I ever thank you, Rex Williamson, for believing in me for over 20 years? You have never said no to me when I asked you to give, print, or champion 54 new church plants. You are an amazing person and friend. Thanks for believing in this project. This book would never be in print without you.

I want to thank my staff and board for encouraging me to finish this writing project that has been on my heart for so long. Thanks to Ken, Steve, Rolland, Teresa, John, Ron, Merle, Scott, and Lloyd. And a very special thanks to Tom and Sch'ree Ward for their unbelievable, constant support over the past ten years. Finally, there are no words to thank you, Gary Kendall, for a lifetime of encouragement. You have been a partner in ministry since we met in our teens. You have walked with me through my successes and my brokenness. Tears are streaming down my face as I try to tell you how much you mean to me. What are the Odds we will be partners until we go to our graves. I'd say about 100 percent. You are the man. I am proud to do life with you. You are truly my best friend.

Preface

My hope and dream for writing this book is simple. I know you have a "What are the Odds" story in your life that could be of great encouragement to others. My hope is that you will take a closer look at your life after reading these stories and see there is a God who is working to bring about good for you. For years, I have referred to Romans 8:28 as the best-loved but most misunderstood verse in the Bible. **"And we know that in all things, God is working to bring about good, for those who love Him and are called according to His purposes."** There are three big misunderstandings to this great verse. The first is that we interpret the verse to mean all things that happen are good and that God is responsible for everything that happens to us. The second is that we overlook the phrase "God is *working!*" I have often wondered how hard God has to work to bring about good, after all of our poor choices. The third misunderstanding is to say that all things work for OUR good. The subject of this passage is not us - the subject is God! IF we would take time to reflect on our lives, we would see how God is working to reveal Himself so we can know Him personally. We would also see how so many great things happen to us - not because of fate - but because a personal God is involved in our lives.

What are the odds God has done some very miraculous things in your life that you have just forgotten or ignored? It happened to the children of Israel. They all followed the cloud by day and cloud of fire by night. They all ate the manna and quail that was provided daily. They saw the Ten Commandments given to Moses, and the water flow from the rock. Then the Grand Daddy of it all was the walk through the Red Sea with walls of water on both sides. They witnessed the Egyptian army being drowned in the sea. What are the odds they would forget these great miracles? What are the odds they would be unfaithful after seeing God care in such a personal way? I'd say about 100 percent. And what are the odds we do the same? About 100 percent.

God is Awesome! What are the odds any of my stories could have happened without a personal God? I think none. What are the odds I will forget and wander from God, if I don't tell these stories to remember God's greatness to me? I think about 100 percent.

I have written this book with the hope of encouraging you to see God at work in your life. I know from sharing my stories over the past couple of years, that 20 or 30 incredible stories have come my way from close friends. These stories have lifted my spirit and my belief that God is a personal God who cares about our daily lives. I am also impressed by how quickly after I tell my stories that people are willing to tell theirs. Would you join this new movement of storytellers? What are the Odds your story could impact someone and bring them back to God? I think about 100 percent!

Let's not be like most of the children of Israel and forget the miracles of God in our lives. Let's not develop a bad case of "spiritual amnesia." Let's be storytellers. Our friends need these stories, our family needs these stories, and our children need these stories. But most of all, I need to tell my own story for me. Wow! What are the odds my own recollection will bring me back to an Awesome God? I think about 100 percent!

Is It Time?

Paul Tee was an *Intel* engineer
                 who had been *transferred* from Malaysia to Phoenix,
and now he and his family were *returning* to Malaysia.
      As I was saying *goodbye*, the last thing I said to Paul was,
            "You will know God cares for you if you meet Neville Tan…
      he is the only person I know who lives in Asia."

         "Where in Asia?" Paul asked.
                        I responded, "Nepal. Is that near Malaysia?"
Paul laughed out loud. "That's what's wrong with you Americans,
         you haven't had the globe out lately.
               I live in the largest city in Malaysia, over a million people,
and we are nowhere near where you are talking about."
               Nepal is at the **top** of India, by Pakistan.

         I was pastor of *Mountain Park Community Church* in Phoenix,
and Paul, Linda, and their two BEAUTIFUL children
                        started *attending* on our very first Sunday.
Soon Linda and the kids had become **regular** attendees,
                  but Paul ONLY attended on SPECIAL days
when the kids were involved in a SPECIAL performance.

                  In those *early* days of the church,
   I didn't have *a lot* of time to visit people in their homes.
                  I often said from up front on Sunday morning.
"If you invite me to your home, I will come
               if you will serve me milk and brownies without nuts."

Linda took me up on the *offer.* She would have me over
and **always** served milk and brownies *without* nuts.

Over our *three-year* relationship, their family and I
developed a **good** friendship. During the third year
of this new church, Linda made a COMMITMENT
to Jesus Christ and was **baptized.**

I stayed *in touch* with the Tee family and through these visits,
I had the **opportunity** to talk to Paul about his life.
One night, after *sharing* about God's love,
I asked Paul if he would like to COMMIT his life to Christ.

His answer **surprised** me. "You are just like my mother."

I wasn't sure if that was a *compliment* or a *complaint.*
I wanted **clarification.** "What do you mean?"

"My mother always asks me, 'Is it time, is it time Paul?'
...meaning is it finally time for me to give my life to Christ."

"Do you welcome her question, or not?" I asked.

His response was **quick** and **emphatic.**
"No...it's never time. I'm an engineer. God doesn't make sense to me."

"Are you more of an agnostic, or an atheist?" I asked.

He seemed INTRIGUED by a question that isn't always *easy* to answer.
"What do you mean?"

"Well, if God would make Himself know to you
or do something big in your life to convince you
that you could trust Him would that make a difference?"

"Something real BIG would have to happen
to convince me." He said **emphasizing** the word "BIG."
He laughed and said, "See, I told you, you are just like my mother."

We both laughed, but then I asked,
"What would it take for you to believe?"

His response was almost the SAME as before, and just as **emphatic.**
"Something BIIIG would have to happen to convince me."
drawing out the word "BIG" with even **more** emphasis than before.

"If you met Neville Tan, would you believe?" I asked.

To this day I have no *logical* explanation for WHY
the name *"Neville Tan"* popped out of my MEMORY BANK,
or **why** that night I asked Paul that question.

And of course, I had to tell him the **little** I knew
of Neville Tan, that I had only heard his name **once**.
My father-in-law, *Oral Withrow*, had told me a story
about him. He had become a missionary in Nepal,
after he had been *released* from prison.
This itself was a **miracle** because Neville Tan had been
given a **life** sentence that was supposedly *non-revocable*.
He had become a Christian in prison, and by some
miraculous means had been *released* from prison.
That was it...ONE story, ONE time, and I'm using
this man Neville Tan to **challenge** Paul Tee
into becoming a Christian just by *meeting* him.

But that was **why**, as we were saying goodbye,
I issued that last CHALLENGE to Paul:
"You will know God exists and cares for you if you meet Neville Tan."

Three months later I RECEIVED an air mail letter
from Linda, and WHAT a story she told.

Linda had been SHOPPING in an outdoor market,
and through a *mutual friend*, had met a woman
who asked her how she was **adjusting** to being back in Malaysia.
Linda told her she was THRILLED to be back,
but she did **miss** her home church in Phoenix.
She *particularly* missed the contemporary *music* and *drama*,
and she missed ME, her pastor.

The woman responded, "You should come to the church
I attend. It sounds a lot like your church in Phoenix.
We have a worship team, a contemporary band
and drama. You should come this Sunday."

She was very *persuasive*, so Linda accepted the invitation,
and Paul **agreed to go** with her.
They LOVED the first part of the service...
the ENERGY was like *Mountain Park Church*,

and Linda felt *God's presence* in a special way
through the *drama* and *worship* team.

After the worship team sat down, a man *moved*
into the pulpit and said, "We welcome you today.
If you are here for the first time,
we give you a very special welcome."
Then he went on to say, "Right now we don't have
a senior pastor, but we have a special guest today
who is a visiting missionary speaker."
What are the odds he would say,
"Our guest is from Nepal, and his name is Neville Tan."

Paul didn't **wait** for Neville to reach the pulpit.
He started *shaking*, and then he stood up, went forward
and *fell* to his knees, sobbing the whole time.
The engineer, who hadn't cried in years, was *weeping*
uncontrollably in the aisle.

Neville Tan didn't know WHAT to think or do.
He came down to Paul, but he couldn't understand
why Paul kept *repeating over and over,*
"My pastor said I would find Neville Tan."
Finally, Linda went forward, and **together**
the two of them *told their story.*

Neville prayed with Paul,
and Paul asked Christ into his LIFE that day.
Years later, they are *back* in the United States
and **still** serving Christ.
I later learned that a REVIVAL started in that church
on that day, and Neville Tan **stayed** there
to pastor the people for a period of time.

So, what are the odds that this man's name
would **pop** into my head that day,
and by only the use of that name, Neville Tan,
Paul Tee's FAITH would be *born* in Malaysia.
As I look back, **the odds are about 100 percent**.

However, there is ANOTHER small plot to this story.
Now, move *forward* a few years...

A friend of mine, Pastor *Rod Stafford* of Fairfax, VA,
called me one night and asked if I had a **good**
missions story that he could *use* when speaking
in Anderson, Indiana, the following Sunday.
The church is *Park Place Church of God*,
a church *vitally* interested in missions,
so I told him the Paul Tee/Neville Tan story.

As he introduced the story, Rod couldn't *resist*
a laugh at my **expense**. He told them,
"Many of you know Robin Wood and you know Robin.
He always has a great story. Sometimes we accuse him of
embellishing just a bit. But the story I tell today
is backed up by an air mail letter.
I have a copy of Linda's letter to prove it."
Rod finished his message with **that** story.

He was *ready* to give an invitation, but **before**
he could get the words OUT, two young men
got *out* of their seats and *walked* toward him.
One of them asked for a *microphone*,
and between the two, they told **this** story:

"We are Neville Tan's sons, and this story
is one of the reasons we now attend Anderson University.
Every detail you just heard is true.
We were with our dad that day, and we will never forget
what happened in that service when Paul Tee came forward."

You can imagine how the church
came **apart** as these two young men spoke.

Again, what are the odds I would *give* Rod this story,
that he would **tell** it at a church where
Paul Tee's *sons* would be IN the audience?
I think about 100 percent!

I have **no** doubt now it was God who *put*
Neville Tan's name on my mind, and that
God **orchestrated** this whole event for Paul Tee.
What are the odds that God wants you to know Him *personally*?
I'd say for you, **the odds are 100 percent!**

A Magical Phone Call

The STRATEGY for planting
this new church was *simple*, yet *profound*.
We would make **23,000** phone calls
in the community of Chandler, Arizona,
and ask **two** questions to every family who answered.
"Are you actively involved in a church?" If they answered YES,
we would thank them and let them know we were
looking to CONNECT with people *without* a church.
If they said NO, we would ask the **second** question,
"Could we send you information about a new church
called, Mountain Park Community Church?"
We never **dreamed** that 2,300 families would say
"NO" to the first question and "YES" to the second.

We began to send *brochures* for 4 weeks in a row
to invite these **2,300** families to the first
Sunday worship service at 10:00 a.m. *October 18, 1987.*
We could NOT have anticipated the personal *impact*
of those phone calls until we met those people
and the *relationships* and *stories* began.

People *always* ask how we made **so** many calls.
It was accomplished with *15 people* a night
making calls for *5 weeks* from a Kole's directory,
from 6:00 p.m. until 9:00 p.m.
Most people we talked to were very *kind* to us,
especially those **without** a church home.
The only ones who were really **tough** on us
were from *Fundamentalist Churches.*

They wondered WHY another church was **needed** besides theirs.

This concept still makes me *chuckle* when I think of Jesus and the religious leaders of His day.

What WOULD happen that first Sunday?

What are the odds anyone would come off of a lone phone call and couple of brochures?

Well, when **305 people** showed up that first Sunday at *Pueblo Middle School*, we were all amazed.

What are the odds we could plant a *thriving* new church at a school with the initials **PMS**? I hope you are smiling.

I wasn't *ready* for a story that first Sunday from Rick and Shelly Wilson, who walked up

to **speak** to me at the close of the service.

They were two of 12 people who decided to COMMIT their lives to Jesus Christ, and what they said **blew me away**.

After praying with them, Shelly began to tell me this story:

"Pastor, I need to tell you what was going on in our home on Thursday night when you

made the phone call. Rick and I were in our living room, he was painting the wall while I was sitting there watching.

I had just lost my mother on Monday, and the following words poured out of my mouth

seconds before you called, 'Rick, what's wrong with us? We don't have a pastor, we don't have a church,

and we don't know God!

What are we going to do for a funeral?'

Rick seemed to not know how to respond, so I repeated myself. 'Rick, we don't have a pastor,

we don't have a church, and we don't know God.

What's wrong with us?' Just then, the phone rang.

When I answered, I heard your voice.

'This is pastor Robin Wood, and we are starting

a new church here in Chandler. I'm wondering if you would answer a couple of questions to help us?'

I covered the phone and said to Rick, 'It's God!'"

I STILL laugh out loud when I picture that scene

with Rick and Shelley. To end the story of that MAGICAL call,

she answered **both** of my questions and gave us *permission*
to send the brochures about our new church.
What are the odds I would be the ONE to call Shelley
right after her phrase about needing a *pastor* and a *church*?
What are the odds God orchestrated the **timing**
of this event? What if I had called the week *before*?
What are the odds of me pointing at THEIR name
and number from over *100,000* names on a Kole's
directory on this *specific* night at this *specific* time?
And what are the odds they would come to
Mountain Park on that opening Sunday?

Of course when God is doing something REALLY
BIG, there is always more to the story.
What are the odds they would tell all of their family
and friends about this special ENCOUNTER?
One of my *favorite* pictures is from our
15th Anniversary celebration at MPCC, of over 35 friends,
family members and children of the Wilson clan.
What are the odds that God orchestrated this one
magical phone call? I think you already **know**
the ANSWER to that question.

100 percent with God!

I Lost It!

The early years of planting *Mountain Park Community Church* were tight for us financially,
so I had to get CREATIVE with ways to
play sports that wouldn't cost me *much* money.
I was very active in athletics, and LOVED
basketball, tennis, and *golf.*
On my days off, I began hitting *golf balls*
in the local park, which was about 175 yards long.
It was the **perfect** place to hit everything
from a wedge to a #6 iron. I continued this until
it was *outlawed* by a city ordinance.
Even today, I take the CREDIT for causing
that community to establish a city code to
eliminate hitting golf balls in the parks!

When I played golf, I always **removed** my
wedding ring because it caused me to get
a *callou*s on the bottom of my ring finger.
One particular day, I finished hitting golf balls
and was heading home when I *realized*
I **hadn't** put my ring back on.
I didn't *panic,* knowing I **always** put my ring
in the bottom pocket of my golf bag.
However, when I got my golf bag out of
the trunk of my car, I was HORRIFIED
to find a **hole** in the bottom of that pocket,
and my ring was **gone**!

I *frantically* looked through the trunk
and on the ground around the car.
I re-traced the park searching *step by step*, but after
a couple of hours, finally **gave up** without any luck.
I was so **desperate** the next morning
I decided to rent a *metal detector*.
I went back and combed EVERY inch of the
grass area where I was, and **still** didn't find the ring.
I felt *sick* inside. I took people with me
to walk the park to look for the ring.
I even prayed. The reason I say, *"even prayed"*
is because we often do *everything*
in our own power **first**, THEN we pray.

I *prayed* a lot over those couple of days,
but prayer **didn't** deliver the ring.
It wasn't the *value* of the ring that hurt,
it was my **wedding** ring, the one *chosen* for me,
and it could NOT be replaced.
It probably only cost a couple hundred dollars,
but it was **worth** a million to me.

Well, I had to **get on** with my life
and the life of this new church.
We sent out a quarterly newsletter in which
I always had an article entitled, *"The Pastor's Perspective."*
I **couldn't** get my mind off the lost ring,
so I wrote about the *sick, sad,* and *desperate* feelings
I had inside about **losing** my wedding ring
while *golfing* at the local park.

As I was writing the article, I felt a **deep** need to
challenge our new church to **care** about lost people
in the same way I had **cared** about my lost ring.
I *reviewed* all that I had done: spending hours *searching*
by myself; *enlisting* other people to help me search;
renting a metal detector; and the most **significant** thing,
spending a lot of time in PRAYER.

I wanted our church to *feel* this same degree
of **desperation** to find those who **didn't** know
a loving God, or have a personal *relationship* with Christ.

I began to write with a **passion**! The article was received well; in fact, it became a *catalyst* for the growth of our church.

What are the odds that a family who
had only *attended* our church **once** would read
my newsletter article, be *moved* by what
I said and come the following Sunday?
At the end of the service, they came *forward*
to talk to me. Their youngest son *approached* me
with his hands closed. He *reached out* to me and said,
"Pastor, I found this in the park. Is it yours?"

He opened his hand, and there was my **wedding ring**!
What are the odds?

His mother added, "We've been praying to find
the person this ring belongs to.
Pastor, God is so good. We prayed to find a church,
and now we know that church is Mountain Park.
God helped us find you, the owner of this ring."

What are the odds that I would FIND my ring?
What are the odds God would use this
experience to help this family **find** a church?

With God, 100 percent again!

Dirk and the Deer

One of the GREATEST joys in my life
has been to **lead** some of my *closest friends* to the Lord.
We can *plant* and *water* the seeds, but it is **up** to God
to bring about the *change* in their lives.

As a young Christian and youth pastor, I began
asking God to *open doors* in the lives of my friends.
I prepared myself as much as I knew how.
I *studied* the Bible, I took *evangelism* training
and I worked at not being **overbearing**
when I talked to people about relationship with God.
I was finally getting the message:
Preparation is **always** good, but the results
will *ultimately* come from God.
God, *not us*, will do the convincing.
So with the words "EXPECT GOD" planted firmly in your mind,
let me now tell you about Dirk and the deer.

I met Dirk and his fiancé Lisa in my early 20's in Eaton, Indiana.
Lisa and her family were *close* friends
and some of my *favorite* people. Dirk and Lisa were about my age,
and it was an **honor** when they asked me to perform their wedding.
Lisa had *committed* her life to Jesus when she was in
the youth group and she was **growing** in her faith.
Dirk was a great guy, he just wasn't **open** to *anything* spiritual.

Dirk and Lisa's *first* home was a log house they built together.
It **fit** the kind of people they were, *particularly* Dirk.
He was *big, strong* and an avid *outdoorsman* and *hunter*.

I thought the timing might be right to SHARE my faith with Dirk
on a visit out to their house one day, but Dirk *very kindly* told me,
"It just doesn't make sense to me." He wasn't being *obstinate*;
he simply felt NO need to make that decision.

I knew it was God's *responsibility* to open Dirk's heart,
not mine. I certainly didn't want to **pressure** him,
but I did decide that it was okay to *challenge* him. So I said,
"Since it is God's responsibility to reveal Himself to you,
would you be willing to ask God to do something
in your life that only God can do?"

This got his *attention*. He didn't answer me,
but his expression said, "Go on, tell me more."
I slightly *rephrased* the question.
"Would you be willing to ask God to do something
for you that only God can bring about?"
I shared with him about how I had a **bad habit**
of *swearing* before I gave my *life* to God.
I asked God to **change** that part of my life.
That seemed to make *sense* to Dirk,

I hugged them both and said, "I love you guys,"
and wished them a good night.

In an ODD sort of way, I think Dirk had decided
to **accept** the challenge, but only on HIS terms.
As I started to walk away, Dirk said,
"I'm going hunting next week.
Would you ask God to give me a deer? A BIG deer."

He was *grinning* from ear to ear because
he'd put it all back on ME.
He was looking to get a *smile* out of me, and he **got** it.

About 10 days later, I got a call from Lisa.
She didn't give **any** particulars but
there was a *definite* urgency in her voice.
"Would you come out to the house?"
"Yeah, I can come tonight." I replied.

When I arrived at their home,
a most *serious* Dirk greeted me.

Lisa wasn't far behind him and she had *tears* in her eyes.

I suspected the **worst**, thinking it was probably
   something going **wrong** in their marriage.
I was almost *afraid* to ask, but I said, "Are you two okay?"
   He quickly dismissed my question
      and started talking about his hunting trip.

"We were hunting for six days with no sign
   of a deer in an area where we had
great success in the past.
   On the last night as we sat around the
campfire it was almost comical.
   We were moaning about our rotten luck,
when we realized that none of us had seen
   any wild game - not even a rabbit or
a squirrel had crossed our path.
   We all headed for our tents but couldn't sleep.
I became obsessed with the challenge
   you had thrown at me, Robin. You said,
'Dirk, God can reveal himself to you if you ask Him.'
   But could He, and would He?
I felt compelled to find out. 'God,' I prayed,
   'please cause a deer to come into this little camp area.
If you show me a deer, I will know
   you are real and that I need you in my life.'
Moments later, I heard a rustling outside my tent.
   I came up on my knees and quietly
unzipped the door flap to look out.
   What are the odds? I could hardly believe
what I was seeing. There stood a deer,
   not more than 10 feet from me. I sat there stunned,
looking the deer in the eye until it turned and walked away."

Dirk was *crying* by this point in the story, when he said,
   "At that very moment I prayed 'God you are for real.'"
Now all *three* of us were in tears. Dirk said,
   "I woke a friend and told him the story, and by flashlight
we were able to find the footprints of that deer."

   I asked Dirk if he wanted to *pray*.
What are the odds...a very quick YES.

Dirk prayed to RECEIVE Christ that night in his home. I'm sure his simple prayer in the tent was *enough*.

What are the odds God will reveal Himself if you ask? What are the odds God will make Himself **known** to those who *truly* seek Him?

"If you seek me, I will be found by you." (1 Chronicles 28:9)

Sounds like 100 percent to me.

The Unlikely Neighbor

After moving to Phoenix, Arizona in July, 1987
to *plant* a church, my family had the privilege
of *choosing* a new home to live in.
We chose a *housing development* just west of I-10.
This community of starter homes for young
families was called *Mountain Park Ranch*,
which was also the TARGET area
for our new church plant.

Of course we *immediately* got acquainted with our *neighbors.*
We *genuinely* cared for the young families
around us and wanted to be **good** neighbors
to them whether they *attended* church or *not.*

This is not a **smart** thing to do, and is even **dumber** to admit,
but as a young pastor, I started trying to *identify*
those who would be the most likely **to** attend
or **not** attend our future church.
Was I ever WRONG about this most of the time!
I had to learn the **hard** way in those early years:
*"God's thoughts are not our thoughts
and His ways are not our ways."* (Isaiah 55:08).

One of the first families to **prove** me wrong about this
was the Grays, Mike and Karen and their children.
At our *first* acquaintance they were **lukewarm** at best.
In my heart, I knew we would NEVER get them
to come to church. But in time,
Karen and my wife became *close friends*,

and my youngest daughter and their
youngest son became **inseparable.**

By the time the church was a *reality,*
Karen and the children began to attend. But not Mike,
who would come very *occasionally* if the children
were doing something **special** in the service.

We gave Mike a SPECIAL invitation to come and hear
a guest speaker, Carma's father, *Pastor Oral Withrow.*
The subject that evening was *"Faith Promise Giving."*

The *concept* in faith promise giving is simple:
participants are *encouraged* to promise
a certain amount of money to missions
and that they will have FAITH God will provide.
This money could be *budgeted,* but the basic idea
is to have FAITH that God will provide a certain amount
of money in ways not yet *known* to the participant,
such as an unexpected raise, an inheritance,
or an unexpected monetary gift.
Anyone *desiring* to do so can sign a non-binding
pledge card showing the amount.
It's all *voluntary,* and the neat part of the deal is
that God is the one who has to come through **first,**
we simply have to be FAITHFUL in passing the money on to missions.

If it hadn't been that the speaker was Carma's **father,**
I'm sure Mike would have REFUSED the invitation.
Mike was an engineer by trade, a very *intelligent* guy,
and he didn't believe that "FAITH STUFF" (his words).
It was probably one of the **worst** scenarios
for Mike to attend a church service on *faith,*
promises, and the *giving of money.*

Oral explained the concept and then
he threw in a *twist* by saying:
"By the way, even if this seems a little crazy,
go home tonight with your spouse and in
separate rooms, privately write down an amount
you think God will provide, then compare.
You just might be surprised to find that

you've both written the same amount."

On the way home, Mike turns to Karen and says,
"That was a real crock. This is what I hate
about church. Crazy belief systems really bug me."

Karen **challenged** Mike.
"Well, why don't we do what he asked?
Let's see if we come up with the same number."

When getting home, they each went into a *separate* room
and stayed for about fifteen minutes.
Karen wrote *$1750* on her piece of paper.
So what are the odds?
Mike had written the exact same amount: *$1750*.

But did that make a **believer** out of Mike? NO!
This could have been a *coincidence* or something,
anything **but** God's doing, according to Mike.

The next morning Mike found an *envelope* on his desk at work.
There was a note which explained his **raise**
from the last year had been MISCALCULATED.
Mike nervously opened the envelope, thinking,
"What if..." And what are the odds,
a check for the **difference** was in the envelope,
the exact amount of *$1750*. God finally had Mike's attention.

Mike began to cry **uncontrollably** at his desk
and didn't know *what* to do.
He went to the restroom for some time,
trying to **calm** himself, but finally *gave up*.
He left a note that said he was ill and headed home.
These emotions were so *unusual* for Mike.
He couldn't **stop** crying all the way home.

When he got home there was **no one** there,
so he walked across the street to our house.
He was STILL crying overwhelmingly and asked for me.
Carma told him I wasn't there, but she invited Mike in
because she could tell he was so **upset**.
He shared his story with her
and she knew she had to **seize** this special moment in time.

I am so **proud** to tell you that she shared
the GOSPEL with Mike in a very simple way
and he prayed to *receive* Christ.

Mike will tell you *neither* he *nor*
his family have been the **same** since.
Because of the **incredible** changes in Mike's life,
over time his *children* came to know Christ also.

So what are the odds of all this? I'd say, 100 percent.

The Eight Quarters

When we were asked to *plant* a church in Chandler, Arizona, we had NO people, NO money, and NO property. The church was just a *dream*. We did have a list of over **90** names of people who indicated *some* interest. I later learned *"some interest"* meant they were glad to know a new church *might* be started and they would like to *meet* the new pastor. Since I have referred to the *Mountain Park Story* earlier in this book, I will only repeat the **vital** details that lead up to this "What are the Odds" story, of a RECONCILIATION that changed my life.

We met with these *interested* 90 people over **5** different desserts at a friend's house in Chandler. After casting the VISION of the new church, I was *inspiring* enough for 12 adults to **sign up** for the DREAM. *Not* quite the number I expected, but like the *Marines*, I was looking for just a few **good** men and women and I had **that**! The first twelve adults not only *signed up*, they gave their *heart* and *soul* to the visionary strategy of making **23,000** phone calls in the "PHONES FOR YOU" campaign. This core team of 12 people, with the help of *North Hills Church* and 20 other faithful volunteers, made 23,000 phone calls in *"The Phones for You"* campaign. Within **four** months of our initial meetings, we scheduled the opening Sunday for *Mountain Park Community Church* to be October 18, 1987 at 10:00 a.m.

I will **never** forget the *promise* and *energy*
of that opening day and how it *unfolded.*
We set up 280 chairs in the school cafetorium.
At 9:55 a.m., I surveyed the room and counted
only **32** people, which included our 12 core members
and the 20 other volunteers who had
helped us with the campaign.
I felt *discouraged* and *beaten.* I said to myself,
"What a bust. This is probably how Moses felt
every time the people voted to go back to Egypt."
I walked out the back door and began to cry out to God,
"Is this the dream? There are thirty-two
phone callers here who already know you!"
I looked at the **name** of the school on the
front bricks, *"Pueblo Middle School,"*
and remembered **once again** that I was starting a church
in a school with the initials **PMS!**

It was at this moment I walked around
the corner of the outside of the school,
and saw cars lined up for nearly a **mile.**
People were parking by the *tens, twenties,*
thirties and *hundreds.* By the time we started
the first morning worship service there were
305 attending *Mountain Park Community Church* for
the first time. At the end of the worship service,
I gave a call for people to make **first time**
commitments to Christ. **Twelve** people responded.
There was ELECTRICITY in the air as the *dream*
had been launched. God was FAITHFUL, and yes,
God cares about **large** numbers.

The next 6 months were a *whirlwind* of unbelievable
things happening with the *growth* and *giving*
at *Mountain Park.* We saw 102 people
make *first time* commitments to Christ,
and averaged **179** people a week. By the end of the first year,
however, *exhaustion* set in. I was going at a **crazy** pace
preaching every week, *singing* on the worship team,
leading a small group, *training* every new leader,
hosting desserts in our home once a week,
and *trying* to raise up a children's and youth ministry.

Desperate for some help and without much *experience* in the area of *staffing*, I reached out and made my first **bad** hire.

Shortly after, I went on a one week vacation to try to *recuperate*. I came back to find my new associate had begun to say I wasn't **ready** to lead a church and wasn't **deep** enough SPIRITUALLY.

Today I can laugh and say, "Of course I wasn't." My reaction was *vulnerable* and *defensive* to those words.

I began to discover something about myself that would **haunt** most of my early ministry: if someone **threatened** the dream of this new church, I went into *combat* mode. It wasn't until years later when taking the *DISC inventory* I would find out my leadership style is highly **Inspirational**, but under *pressure*, I resort to **Dominance**. Being young and **not** in touch with my personality type, I responded very **defensively** with an *Apostle Paul and Barnabas experience* recorded in Acts 15.

The new associate and I **split** company and he *left* - with **40** people, most of our *original* core group, and about **60 percent** of the church income. I experienced the *loss* of people from a church because of ME, for the first time in my ministry.

During the next 4 years, I would experience this **trauma** another *4* or *5* times. I began to believe I had the SPIRITUAL gift of losing **40** people at a time! The church would grow another **150** or so and then a group would feel *neglected* and **leave**. I kept hearing, "All Robin cares about is more people," or "You just aren't deep enough, we aren't being fed." Because I was a *fighter* and a *survivor*, the church continued to **grow**, but deep inside I felt *empty*. I had lost a number of people I **loved** and had poured my life into. Things looked *okay* on the surface and we were running near **400**, but the *joy* had been **sucked** out of my life.

It all came to a **head** in a board meeting going into our 5th year. I remember *sitting* in this meeting and feeling *blind-sided* by the conversation.

One of the leaders expressed he thought I had a **personal** problem with people. We had just let a staff person go for *infidelity*, but the conversation was about ME not handling it **correctly**.

This led to me to ask each board member if they thought my ministry should **continue** or **not**.

I'm a pastor's kid, and one thing I've learned from my dad and other great pastors over the years, is that without FULL support of your board, you just CAN'T lead *effectively*. Your main leaders have to be **behind** you. So I asked each of them to share whether they thought I *should* be the pastor of our church or not.

One of the most **painful** experiences in my life took place in the next 30 minutes.

Four of the members said my ministry was OVER, and 4 said "I want you to be my pastor."

When the ninth member, Marcus began speaking, I was looking down and had already decided to **resign**.

At that moment it didn't matter that he said quite a few **kind** words about me *changing* his life and his family and that he very much *wanted* me to be the pastor.

As the meeting ended, I walked outside with Marcus and told him I would be **resigning** the next day.

He asked me if I would go and see his father, *Dr. Ralph Earle*, a counselor and former pastor.

Marcus stressed, "I really think he could help you. I think you need help with your anger issues and the pain in your extended family."

The next day I sat in Dr. Earle's office. I began to **pour out** my personal story, beginning with the meeting the previous night.

I must have **cried** for half an hour, but I began talking for the **first** time about my personal *pain* and *issues* in my life.

I met with Dr. Earle **several** more times before doing an **intensive** session with him and Marilyn Murray, author of the book *"Prisoner of Another War."*

During this three-day session, I put **everything** out
on the table. I shared about the *deep hurt*
of **losing** people I loved. I talked about those
who I had given my *life* to, the first 12 adults
and how I so much *wished* they were in my life.
I talked about the **brokenness** in my personal
family with my brother and sister and my parents.
I talked about the **pain** of making such a small
amount of money as a pastor and not being able
to take care of my family *financially.*
I was like a fire hydrant; it all **gushed** out.
A *healing process* started to take place in
my life, with great REALIZATIONS about
my *defensive tendencies* and *leadership traits.*

I went back to my leaders and shared about
my own **brokenness** and repented first to them.
Then we talked about doing church *differently.*

What are the odds, my neighbor Mike Gray,
would come over one night and ask me to attend
a special service with him at *North Hills Church.*
To make a long story short, I held some *resentment*
towards this church because of what I perceived
as a broken commitment made to me and my family.
Initially I *didn't* want to go, but my counseling experiences
had **empowered** me to not be so *defensive.*
I was *hesitant,* but I made the 45 minute drive north
to a special service with a man named Ray Bringham.
I wasn't **prepared** for the worship service
I was about to *experience.* I sat on the back row
and we sang for about 30 minutes.
I remember wondering if it would **ever** end,
and thinking I wasn't getting **anything** out of it.
Then Ray got up and began by saying,
"I'm not going to preach today. I just want to
ask all of you to open your heart
to repentance, prayer, and reconciliation."

I thought to myself, "I can't believe I came
all this way and there's no message."

I had *never* met Ray, and without
dishonoring this man I love so much now,
I thought he was a bit *quirky* and not very *inspirational.*
He began by saying he simply wanted us
to be **open** to what God would **do** in our lives
if we would *pray, repent,* and *seek* God's face.
I could **never** have *anticipated* what would happen next.
He asked people to stand who needed to REPENT
of anger in their life. Pretty simple. **No one stood,**
so Ray asked if anyone would *raise* their hand.
I wasn't going to be the *first.* But soon, a number
of hands went up and Ray very gently said,
"If someone is raising their hand near you,

just go and place your hand on their shoulder
and pray for them to be delivered."

A **number** of people began doing this.
Then Ray continued to *expand* this time of REPENTANCE.
I don't remember *every* area he asked for repentance in,
but I **do** remember him asking for people to stand
or raise their hand if they had **not** been tithing
by giving **10 percent** of their income.
I thought, *"No one is going to repent of this."*
But I was *overwhelmed* when at least 10 people stood.
Once again, Ray asked people to *pray* for those
standing to be released and to be *faithful*
in this area of repentance. Then Ray asked for spouses
to REPENT to each other if they had *bitterness.*
WOW! I was amazed as over **20** couples walked forward.
Once again, Ray simply asked for people
to come and lay hands on them and pray
for *reconciliation* to happen in these marriages.
Then Ray closed with,
"If you need to ask someone here to
forgive you for your attitude toward them,
I want you to get up and go to that person.
If you've hurt someone in this church,
I want you to go and repent to that person right now."

I was sitting on the back row,
feeling pretty *comfortable* watching others repent.

Suddenly, a woman I knew named Rhonda
                walked *straight up* to me. She and her husband Randy
were part of one of the groups of people who had left
                Mountain Park and expressed **disappointment** with me.
        I remember being so **hurt** after feeling
                I had really **been there** for this family.
    I met Randy in prison and had *led* him to Christ,
                and I loved Rhonda and their children.

    Rhonda walked up to me, *knelt down* at my feet,
                and began to *cry* and *beg* me for FORGIVENESS.
I hugged Rhonda and asked her to get up,
                because I needed to ask **her** forgiveness
    for the *bitterness* in my heart toward her and her family.
            WOW! My world had experienced *repentance*
        and *reconciliation* at the **highest** level.

        I remember the feeling of *healing* and *wholeness* even today.
We offered each other FORGIVENESS
                with **no** strings attached, quite an emotional experience.
    The service lasted about two and half hours
                and then Mike and I drove home *rejoicing*.
I'll *never* forget we stopped for a *Marie Calendar's*
                cherry pie to **celebrate** what God had done that night.
For the next few days, the **joy** I had lost
                was returned to me **100-fold**.

            Later that week, Mike asked me the BIG question,
"Can we have Ray come to our church to hold
                services on 'Ten Days of Prayer and Repentance'?"
        I was a little *nervous* about Ray and his approach,
                but something big had happened.
    I didn't know how to **explain** all of this to my
                leadership board but they *listened* to me and Mike
and *opened* their heart to the ten day experience.

        Ray came to *Mountain Park* for **two** consecutive
Sundays and brought an *unbelievable*
                outpouring of God's power of FORGIVENESS
through *repentance* and *prayer* for a ten day period.
                We had people *sign up* to come to the church
to pray *around the clock* for ten days.

On the first Sunday, Ray did his *thing*. He got up,
didn't preach, but simply *asked* people to repent
in the same way he did at *North Hills*.
To my **amazement**, our people in this new church,
without much of a church background,
responded unbelievably. The first Sunday,
over **20** people *repented* for **not** tithing,
and 25 married couples *repented* to each other.
People let go of BITTERNESS and ANGER, *repented* to me
personally for **not** praying for me daily as their pastor,
and some *repented* for feelings of **anger** that happen
in every church between pastors and leaders.
The place came APART.

Not *everyone* appreciated Ray's **boldness**, and I had
several calls the following week from leaders who
were very *uncomfortable* with the VULNERABILITY
being created. By Friday, however, I knew God was doing
such **good** work in my personal life through
REPENTANCE that I wanted to speak on it.
Little did I know that God would *wake* me up at 2 a.m.
that Sunday and *impress* upon me something to do
before the church service that would *change*
my life **forever**. I couldn't get back to sleep.
All I could think about was God **urging** me
to *repent* to a number of people I had **hurt**
when they *left* the church in our first year.

I made a list of *eight* families on my heart
and wrote down their phone numbers.
Then I found *8 quarters* and drove to a
convenient store on the corner of *48th* and *Warner*.
I'm not sure WHY I didn't just make the calls
from **home**. I think I was *afraid* to even tell
my wife what I was doing.
I was also *afraid* most of these people would
just hang up on me. But what are the odds,
God was at work in a very **special** way.
I got a hold of **7** of the 8 families, and all
but **one** of those people let me *come* to their
house that morning and *repent* to them personally.

The one man who **didn't** let me come to
                    his house was John Gutierrez, who said,
        "Robin you can't come to me, because
            I am going to come to you to repent."

WOW! John showed up for the *first* worship service,
                where we fell into each other's arms *repenting*.
He got up and spoke about what the phone call
                had meant to him, after which more people *responded*
and came forward to *repent* of bitterness in their life.
                        Then I shared about making the 8 phone calls
        and the visits I made that morning.
                        There were many *tears of joy, repentance,*
        and **healing** in peoples' lives.

What are the odds there is one more **huge** twist
                    to the story. Remember I contacted 8 families
        but was unable to reach one of them.
                        Number **8** was Merle and Susan Turner.
In our beginning years, Merle had become my personal
                    doctor, and Susan was a **great** influence to my kids.
We had *brokenness* between us and they were
                    among the first 40 that **left** our church.
I had a huge *emptiness* in my heart over this
                    broken relationship. But when I dialed the Turner's
        number that morning, it had been *disconnected*.
                    I was *disappointed* but thought I would just
        try to contact them that week.

        The first service ended and the place was **electric**
with God's presence. I was walking out to greet
                        those arriving for the second service when I saw
        two familiar faces - Merle and Susan Turner -
                who I had not seen in **over 3** years.
        Sometimes I am *really* slow to understand
                    God's MIRACULOUS power, and I exclaimed,
            "What are you two doing here!"

    They asked if they could talk to me *privately*.
                        What are the odds, Susan was *awakened*
    by a dream that they should come to *Mountain Park*
                    on Sunday. They had NO idea what had

been *happening* over the past ten days
with *prayer* and *repentance*. Merle had said to her,
"Are you sure?" And Susan responded,
"Yes, God wants us to go to
Mountain Park and repent to Robin."
We all broke into *tears* and held each other,
and they got up to *share* the story
of RECONCILIATION in the second service.

What are the odds that all of this could have happened
without God? I believe a ZERO percent chance.
Merle and Susan returned to *Mountain Park* and
became one of the *lead givers* to the first building fund.
Our relationship remains **changed** to this very day.
Merle serves on our board at the *Church Multiplication
Association* and is **still** my personal physician.

God brought the **joy** of my ministry back *ten-fold.*
What are the odds God would use
eight quarters to **change** my life?
What are the odds all of this would be a *chain reaction*
beginning with the **"Unlikely Neighbor"** Mike,
inviting me to a church service?
What are the odds Rhonda's *willingness* to reconcile
with me would lead to me RECONCILING with 8 families?
What are the odds it takes just one FAITHFUL person
to start a chain of events that will *affect* thousands?

This story was told *over* and *over* again
in the life of our church for the next 14 years.
It so reminds me of the woman who *broke* the jar
of perfume to ANOINT Jesus' feet, and Jesus said,
"Everywhere the gospel is preached, the story of
this one woman's act of faithfulness will be told."
It all began with Rhonda *kneeling* at my feet
and asking for FORGIVENESS.

What are the odds God might want to begin
a *chain reaction* like this with you?
I'd say about One Hundred Percent!

The Principle of One

Long *before* I met Laura Lee and Eugene
and the homeless communities of Phoenix,
I had *volunteered* to speak weekly at the
homeless shelter in Casper, Wyoming. I grew to **love**
those men and *Elmer Mutchler*, the director.

As I became *more* involved with the ministry,
I became *more* acutely aware of the shelter's daily needs:
more money, *more* pastors for nightly speaking
and *more* well-equipped persons on the board.

As soon as God brought these needs to my mind,
I had another *sobering* thought:
"Robin, you have already been gifted with the
abilities to find the right people to fill these needs."

By the time I left Casper, there were key persons on the board,
enough speakers for every night and *enough* financial support.
The *Gospel Rescue Mission* in Casper was **thriving**
when it came time for me to *leave* Casper
to plant a church in Phoenix, Arizona.
I got so *wrapped up* in the many aspects of starting
the new church in Phoenix, that I totally **neglected**
my PASSION for the homeless ministry.
However, through a set of *unique* circumstances,
I would meet Laura Lee and Eugene.
I think I can *honestly* say God used Laura Lee to **change**
my life and the ministry of *Mountain Park Community Church*.

Our church had a ministry of giving household furnishings
            to families in need. In *October of 2001* a missions team
from our church was delivering furniture to a
            single mom's apartment. I noticed a thin, possibly middle-aged
woman just hanging around, watching us.

                "Why are you giving her furniture?"
she finally worked up the NERVE to ask.
                    "Our church tries to provide basic needs
        to families in the community" I told her.

After looking at me for a minute, she stated,
                very *matter-of-factly*, "I could use some help."

I introduced myself and found out her name was Laura Lee.
                        "Where do you live, Laura Lee?"
    She totally **ignored** my question and said
                    "My teeth hurt all the time."
    "How bad do they hurt?"
        "I have extreme pain all the time," she repeated.

Our church had already developed a FREE ministry
                with a team of doctors and dentists, so I asked her:
"Would you be willing to see my dentist, Dr. Farran?"

        She agreed and we *set up* a time within the next couple of days.

"Where do you live?" I asked her again. "I need your address."
                    She pointed to some *mountain buttes* just behind
the apartment complex. "I don't have an address. I live outside."

        I was **blown away**. I wasn't *naive*. I knew there were homeless
living outside, but I didn't know any *personally*.
    In Casper, the homeless men I worked with were **inside** a shelter.
Here, Laura Lee was *pointing* to a butte, telling me,
                    "Meet me on the top of that little mountain."
    "So, what should I do"? I asked.
            "Just climb up the path on the south side
and you will find our camp on the top of the third level.
                    Eugene really likes the third level," she said.
    "Who is Eugene?" I asked.
            "He's the guy I've been with for the past 10 years.
Don't be afraid. He'll have a machete,
        but I'll tell him who you are and everything will be O.K."

This was to be my **invitation** into the world
of *dumpster-diving* and *living under bridges*,
on top of buttes and in alleys.
In fact, anywhere the homeless could
throw down a sleeping bag or *build* a primitive
shelter of tin, tent or cardboard.
This was a *sub-culture* of people that I would fall
in love with and minister over the next four years.

At 9:00 a.m., two days after I met Laura Lee,
I was climbing toward the top of the third level,
clutching my cell phone with my finger on speed dial
just in case I needed help *quickly*.
I was calling out, "Laura Lee, Laura Lee."

All of a sudden a warrior, wielding a **machete,**
bolted from his self-made camp and started for me.
I found out *later* Laura Lee had
forgotten to tell Eugene I would be there.

I threw both hands in the air, walking backwards.
"Hey, it's me...Pastor Robin. Where's Laura Lee?"

Hearing me, she came out from under their rigged
awning and SHOUTED out to Eugene.
"Eugene, it's Pastor Robin. I forgot to tell you
I was going to the dentist today."
I held out my hand and *officially met* Eugene,
but Eugene didn't **trust** me. After he heard about
a *free* dentist, he didn't trust him either.
He INSISTED on going with us.
At least he **left** the machete at the camp.

During the 25-minute ride, Eugene had lots of questions,
but they always came back to wondering,
"Why would a dentist work for free?"
"Dr. Farran is one of the kindest men I know,"
I kept telling him. "He helps lots of people
who don't have the money to pay."
This was a totally *foreign* concept to Eugene.

After Dr. Farran had seen Laura Lee, he told me,
"Robin, you could not even be walking around

with the pain raging in her mouth.
She has 20 cavities and her gums are filled with infection.
She hasn't seen a dentist in her entire life."

At church on the following Sunday morning,
I **shared** about my *experience* with Laura Lee and her teeth.
What are the odds, right after service, a young man
named Greg, who was skilled in making dentures,
volunteered to make some for Laura Lee?
In fact, he began a *new ministry* in our church
of gifting dentures to the poor.
He taught us all at MPCC that *whatever* you
do *well*, you can **give** away.

During the next four years, MPCC became involved in
a ministry to the homeless that **changed** the church
as much as it *changed* the lives of the homeless.
And all of this happened because of our
relationship with Laura Lee and Eugene.
We had doctors and dentists GIVING their time.
We helped families *find jobs* and *apartments*;
we got children *vaccinated* and we picked up
the homeless in their communities
and took them to church and to dinner afterwards.
We **provided** home furnishings and food when needed.
Our ministry to this hidden *sub-culture* was one
of the reasons *Mountain Part Community Church*
became a GREAT church.

However, the **two major obstacles**
the homeless fight are *drugs* and *mental illness*,
with mental illness taking the **heaviest** toll.
This is the reason most homeless stories don't end *happily*.
The mentally ill don't have the **ability** to
continue caring for themselves, and those addicted
to drugs don't have the **willpower** to stop.

The rate of success is **extremely** low,
and often we Christians are asked,
"Why do you even bother? You can't change them."

But we operate on Jesus' **principle of the one.**

Over 36 times in the New Testament,
Jesus takes time for THE ONE.
Three of the most magical stories in the Bible
are about the shepherd who leaves 99 sheep
that are safe, to save the one who is lost;
the woman who searches until she finds the lost coin;
and the story of the prodigal son and loving father.
It's the principle of one that grabs my heart.

Then, Jesus says, *"When you do for one of the least of these,*
you are doing it for me."

It was this **principle of one** that caused us to BELIEVE
Laura Lee and Eugene could find a BETTER life.
We helped Eugene find a *job* in the building industry.
They both became Christians and I will **never** forget
the joy of performing their wedding on a
Sunday morning at *Mountain Park.*
For a while life really **changed** for Laura Lee and Eugene.

It still *grieves* me to think of Eugene going **back**
to the world of drugs. Laura Lee **wouldn't** leave him.
In 2004 when I was moving to Oklahoma City,
I was made aware that they were living **back** under
a bridge in downtown Phoenix.
I went to say goodbye to them and what I found
broke my heart. I *climbed* down to where they
were camped and gave them both *tight hugs.*
Eugene was somewhat **belligerent**,
but Laura Lee was *genuinely glad* to see me.
On leaving, I held her and *prayed* with her,
asking God to help her be the person He had **called** her to be.
I made her **promise** she would come back
to her FAITH in Jesus, even if she had to leave Eugene
and his *addiction* to drugs.

As I left that **desperate** situation, I prayed
"Please don't let all that we have done
and their miracle be all for nothing."
I didn't know if I would EVER see Laura Lee again.
In February 2007 I was asked by *North Hills Church*
to consult them in finding a new pastor.

I agreed to speak for 7 weeks leading up to Easter Sunday.
We decided to do a mailer in the community to
30,000 homes to invite people to the Easter celebration.
My picture was on the brochure and the
message was entitled *While It Was Still Dark*.
The text referred to the fact that *Mary Magdalene*
went to the tomb while it was still dark.
I used this text to *emphasize* that many people
don't seek God **until** their lives become *very* dark.

I had *finished* speaking at the first service
and was greeting people at the door when
a *familiar* looking woman with a weatherworn face
walked towards me. What are the odds I thought?
"Could it be Laura Lee?"
She **threw** her arms around me and said
"I've prayed for three years to see you again."
She was *clutching* the brochure we had sent
to the 30,000 homes. What are the odds?
Not only had God **answered** her prayer,
it was most *significant* to me that God had **brought** her back
on the very Sunday that I was speaking on *Mary Magdalene's*
DELIVERANCE from her lifestyle.

I'm not sure WHY, but I somehow had always *associated*
Laura Lee's story with the story of *Mary Magdalene*.
Here she was, telling me God had given her the **power** to leave Eugene.
I had never seen her in so much PEACE.

I **immediately** asked if she would tell her story at the second service.
She did, and the place came apart. WOW!

So what are the odds that the **principle of one**
would be at work for Laura Lee 14 years **after** I met her?

I'd say about 100 percent.

Modern Day Fishes and Loaves

When I moved to Phoenix Arizona in 1987,
I not only wanted to *plant* a new church,
         but I wanted to be a *part* of the community.
   I absolutely LOVE sports, so I jumped at the *opportunity*
                          to **coach** a YMCA basketball team when my
8 year old son Brady decided he wanted to *play*.
            At this time we had lived in Phoenix for three years,
      and little did I know, this would be one of the **greatest** ways
                   to *meet* new families in the area.

   I was given a *handfu*l of eight-year-old boys
                  to **teach** what I knew. I had *played* college basketball
and didn't know HOW I'd teach basketball from scratch,
                   but I **loved** those kids and gave it my best.
         During the early 90's, the *Phoenix Suns*
                        were building a **powerhouse** team.
      Had Michael Jordan NOT been born, we might have
                  had a **few** banners hanging in *U.S. Airways Arena*.
      Because these 10 young boys **idolized** the *Suns*,
            I called each of them by one of the *Sun's* names.
   We **never** won a lot of games, but I truly *enjoyed*
                     teaching them the sport I **loved** so much.

It was through *coaching* this basketball team I met
                     Brian and Connie Harrison and their two boys.
   Their youngest son, Eric, played on our team,
            and after spending some time with them as Eric's coach,
their family *began* to attend our new church.
            Mountain Park was involved with Chuck Colson's

Angel Tree Ministry from the first year we were established.
Buying **gifts** for prisoner's kids and then delivering
them had **touched** our church at a high level.
At one point, we were giving gifts to **over 300** prisoner's kids.
We caught Chuck Colson's TOTAL VISION of staying in
relationships with as many families as we could
throughout the year. We tried our best to make it much
MORE than just a "FEEL GOOD" ministry around Christmas.

A woman by the name of Karen Gray began to tutor
some children she had developed a relationship with
through *Angel Tree*. She came to me one week
and shared that the 5 children
she was tutoring **didn't** have bicycles.
She wondered if our church could **buy**
these kids bikes. It wasn't a HUGE request financially,
so I said **sure**. However, I cannot *explain* how all week
I kept having the thought,
"Why not ask for 5 bikes on Sunday morning in church?"

That was the **way** we did things at *Mountain Park,*
not with the *intention* of trying to save money,
but to give someone an *opportunity* to be
involved in *giving* and *touching* someone's life.
So, I ASKED the church that Sunday morning
in the first service for 5 bikes
I wasn't **prepared** for what happened after the service.

Brian and Connie Harrison walked up the
middle isle with their youngest boy, Eric.
Brian looked me in the eye and said,
"Our son has something to tell you Coach."

Eric looked right in my eyes and said,
"Coach, I want to give my new bicycle
that I got for my birthday yesterday."

WOW! Brian and Connie said they
were *willing* to let him do this.
They were not **believers** yet, but felt Eric
was doing something VERY important.
Little did any of us know how SPECIAL this moment
would be in the *life* of our church.

During the second service, I asked for **4** bikes
and told the story of what had happened
after the first service when Eric
decided to give his new birthday bike.
At the end of the service, I told people they could
drop off the bikes they wanted to give
at my garage, *4213 E. Briarwood Terrace.*
It was an *emotional* day,
highlighted by the **gift** of Eric's bike.

A woman visiting the church for the first time
came to me after the service and said very simply,
"Take this business card, I have a feeling
you are going to get more than 5 bikes today.
If you do, give Bill Merrit a call."

I placed the card she handed me
in my coat pocket and thanked her.
What are the odds that by 3 pm that afternoon
I had **153** bikes delivered to my garage.
I was overwhelmed at the GENEROSITY of our people
and couldn't believe what was happening.
That evening I remembered the card in my pocket
and called Bill Merrit, a man I had *never* met,
and told him what had happened. Without telling
me anything else, he invited me to his home.
He asked me to please come *immediately.*

I drove to Bill's house, where he took me
back to his garage and opened the door.
Inside, there were about **30** bikes hanging from the
ceiling and a work area where he restored the bikes.
He told me a story I will **never** forget.
"Last year, I was asked to restore 50 bikes to give
to 50 very poor children through a charity.
However, when I went to the event, there were 200
kids without bikes. They counted out every 4th kid
by saying 1-2-3-4: you get a bike; 1-2-3-4: you get a bike."

Bill told me he fell apart emotionally when he saw
150 kids leave that place without a bike.

Then he asked me, "Can I partner with you to never let
this happen again? I can't get to 200 bikes without your help."

I *invited* Bill to my church the next week and we SHARED
about the 153 bikes and the **need** for more bikes.
What are the odds God was up to something that
would become known as the *Bike Ministry at MPCC*.
And what are the odds something else was about to happen?
At the close of the service, I asked people to COMMIT
their lives to Jesus Christ. **Guess** who made a commitment?
Bill and Cathy Merrit. WOW! What are the odds?
I'd say with God, about 100 percent.

Over the next 10 years, we PARTNERED with Bill Merrit
to give over *2,000* bikes, making sure every child
involved with that charity got a **bike** for Christmas.

Does this story **remind** you of a little boy in the Bible
who brought a couple fish and a few loaves to Jesus
when they were trying to gather food for **5,000** people?
Jesus *took* what that little boy *gave* and **multiplied** it
to meet the need. We were experiencing
a similar MIRACLE right before our very eyes.
Eric, this little eight-year-old boy had
brought his new bike and now Jesus was
multiplying his gift to reach thousands.

What are the odds God was doing something VERY special
in Eric's heart? What are the odds God wanted to
birth a bike ministry at MPCC?
What are the odds God wanted Bill and Cathy to
find Christ and a church through this **experience**?
What are the odds that God needed a church to be
broken by a child in order to help hundreds of adults **'Get It?'**
What are the odds God wants you to LET GO of something
materially so he can **multiply** it a hundred fold?

I'd say about 100 percent.

Hi, My Name is Robin
and I'm a Sports Addict

This is a story of PERSISTENCE,
with some **craziness** woven in.
During the late 80's and early 90's,
I developed a *friendship* with a very special
person who was **connected** to the **NBA**.
The relationship began with a
"What are the odds" experience at *Mountain Park*.
We were in our fourth year as a church plant when
I went through a *difficult* time in my personal life
and entered *counseling* with Dr. Ralph Earle.

Dr. Earle is a *world-renown* counselor
specializing in **addictions**. In my first session,
I declared I **didn't** have any addictions.
Of course I was thinking of *alcohol, tobacco,*
and any habit-forming *drugs,* which was my
understanding of addictions at the time.
I was raised in a CONSERVATIVE church
where we had the old saying,
"I don't smoke, drink or chew, or go with girls who do!"
A cute little line, but **narrow** in the realm
of dealing with *addictions* people face every day.

After some intense *self-disclosure* sessions dealing with
my *family-of-origin* issues and doing a trauma egg
and family tree, I realized I had a number of
possible addictions. Unfortunately, these addictions

would be seen by the church as ACCEPTABLE.

No one will **accuse** you of having a *sports* addiction just because you watch *Sports Center* three times in a row – but do you know how SICK that practice is? It's the **same** show and the **same** highlights.

If you can't get to sleep *without* watching the T.V., no one will would call that an **addiction**.

If you eat **sugar** incessantly, you most likely won't be accused of having a *sugar addiction*. If you *shop till you drop* every weekend, people will smile and act like it is **normal**. If you **eat** to fill a hole in your heart, no one will accuse you of a *food addiction*. There are MANY addictions **destroying** people's lives that we readily accept as **normal**, which I call *"acceptable addictions."*

Dr. Earle and I later discovered my *primary* problem was an **Adrenaline** addiction. I preached from *adrenaline*, competed from *adrenaline*, and would do normal tasks of cleaning around the house and loading the dishwasher with my *adrenaline* kicked in high gear.

I had a *sports* addiction that engaged my *adrenaline* addiction, and both were **destructive** to my life.

Addictions of ANY kind **ruin** relationships because a person will ALWAYS choose the *rush* over *relationships*.

Discovering this *problem-area* of my life **saved** me in many ways.

But what are the odds my addiction would lead me to a **great** friendship? One Sunday morning I was speaking about my own issues as a *sports* addict and *adrenaline* addict. It was the opening message of a 12-step series on dealing with addictions. I shared OPENLY with my congregation about my own *struggle* with these addictions, then *challenged* them not to be fooled by the **subtle** addictions that could *ruin* their lives. When Paul expresses his *struggle with sin* in Romans 7, his words sound like an **addict**. "I do not understand what I do, but what I hate I do. And if I do what I do not want to do, I agree that the law good. As it is, it is no longer I myself who do it,

but it is sin living in me. I know that nothing good
lives in me, that is, in my sinful nature.
For I have the desire to do what is good,
but I cannot carry it out.
For what I do is not the good I want to do;
no, the evil I do not want to do, this I keep on doing.
Now if I do what I do not want to do, it is no longer
I who do it, but it is sin living in me
that does it." (Romans 7:15-20)
That sounds like an **addict** talking to me.

When people *challenge* me and say,
"Robin you speak as if we all have addictions!"
I simply respond, "The Bible says we all have sinned
and fallen short of the glory of God." (Romans 3:23)
I don't know a verse that says it **better**.
"ALL HAVE SINNED!" We all have a
sinful nature and I am *comfortable* with
understanding that this is an *addiction* to sin.
So I want to ask you, what is your sin addiction?

After **pouring** my heart out to our church family
about my *own* life, I went to the door after the service
to shake hands. I was met by a *particular* gentleman who
thanked me for the message. I looked at his face and said,
"I know you!"

He said, "You might know my face, but you won't know
my name unless you are truly a sports addict!"
I responded, "You are Ed Rush, an NBA referee!"

I will NEVER forget when he said, "You really are an addict!
If you know the name of the referees in the NBA you need help!"

We both *laughed* and planned a lunch together.
What are the odds, on the day I admitted
publicly to my *addiction* to sports,
that I would have it CONFIRMED completely?
This started a **great** friendship, which would lead
to a couple of little "What are the odds" stories
in my travels with Ed Rush.
Ed would **often** take me with him to games in Phoenix.
The CATCH was I had to *ride* with him to the arena,

---

where we would go to the *locker room*
and get a *neck pass* for media persons.

One day I was *anxiously* looking forward
to meeting Ed for a **playoff** game,
when I got a phone call about a man
in our church having a *heart attack*.
Of course Ed couldn't **wait** for me
because he was the *lead official*. I **pleaded** with him,
"Ed can I come to the game later?"

Ed responded, "If you find a way in the arena,
come down to the floor and I'll give you
the media pass to wear around your neck."

I laughed out loud at my SHALLOWNESS as I drove
to the hospital thinking, "Why don't people check
with my schedule before having a heart attack?"
After *praying* with the man from MPCC,
everything looked **good**, and I *jumped* back
in my car and **rushed** to the arena.

I wondered if I should try to **scalp** a ticket to get in,
but in those days, there weren't ANY cheap tickets.
The *Phoenix Suns* were the **hot item** in town.
You would have to cough up at least **$100** bucks
for a seat in the **upper** deck.
It was the *glory days* of Charles Barkley,
Kevin Johnson, and Tom Chambers.
This was the year we **battled** Michael Jordan
and the *Chicago Bulls* for the **NBA title**.

With very **little** money in my pocket, I began to walk
from *gate to gate*, hoping someone would **believe** my
truthful story that I was a pastor who **knew** the *lead referee*
but was *late* to the game because of a hospital visit.
As I talked with each *gate person*,
I couldn't even get **half** my story out without
them all saying something along the lines of,
"Sir, please move on, we can't just let you go in."

Being a **persistent** sports fanatic, I kept going
for about **20 gate**s until I was finally *weary*.

Have you ever been SO ready to **give up**,
yet something inside you says, "Try one more time."
I wanted to **give up**, but that small voice **shouted**,
"Try one more gate."

What are the odds I would try ONE more time,
and as I walked up to the young woman
working the gate, I *recognized* her face.
What are the odds it was Heather,
who had attended *Mountain Park*,
where her entire family had given their *lives* to Christ?
When Heather saw my face, she exclaimed,
"Pastor, why are you so late to the game?"
"You won't believe my story tonight," I said, exhausted.
"Try me," she said. "I love your stories."

After I'd *recapped* my night, even though
she **believed** me, she whispered in my ear,
"I could lose my job if I let you in without a ticket."
I told her when I got in I would get my
media pass and come back and **show** her.
She agreed, and opened the gate.
I couldn't **believe it** - I was actually IN!

It was *halftime* and I made my way down to
the court to find Ed. I called out his name and he
turned around with a huge smile on his face.
"I've got money on you finding your way
in to this game! Tell me the story!"
He called over his fellow referee Dick and said,
"Meet my pastor. I told you he would talk his way in."
I had so much **fun** telling them the story,
and he placed the *media pass* around my neck.

What are the odds you need to **believe** that
the *persistent* voice inside you saying,
"Just try one more time," is God's voice?
What are the odds God wants you to try
something **again**, one more time?
What are the odds that voice is *asking* you
to **trust** God once more with your marriage,
your kids, or your calling?
I think they are 100 percent!

Miracle on 24th Street

By the end of my 17 years as pastor
of *Mountain Park Community Church*,
there were over 5,000 people in Phoenix
who called MPCC their home church.

As I mentioned earlier, there are *countless* untold
"what are the odds" stories about MPCC, however,
there are two I believe BEST illustrate how God
was involved in **all** the details, both *large* and *small*,
of the LIFE and GROWTH of this church.
The naming of the church is the *first* story,
and when you know the *second* story, you will see
how far **ahead** God was AT WORK
when we chose the name.

I should say when THEY chose the name.
I had already decided on what I considered a FRESH,
yet STRONG name: *New Covenant Community Church*.
This name had a **vibrant** message for the
rapidly-growing community of Chandler, Arizona.
I could tell about God's "NEW AGREEMENT"
with us through His son, Jesus Christ.
I lobbied **hard** to convince the other 11 people in our
core group that this was the IDEAL name.

But this was NOT to be the name.
What I **didn't** count on was competing
with someone's *dream* from God.
Would you **believe** a woman named Susan Turner

had a dream so VIVID that as she told it in detail,
she **convinced** all our core members we should name
the church *Mountain Park Community Church*?
To me, it was **ridiculous**. We were meeting in a middle school
that was 12 miles from the Phoenix community of
Mountain Park Ranch. That name would be fitting
for a church THERE, but **not** where we located in Chandler.

But how do you **compete** with a *dream* from God?
I lost an 11 to 1 vote, and there was NO hope in changing
anyone's mind. Even those **closest** to me *defected*.
Sure enough, *"Mountain Park Community Church"*
was the name chosen. What are the odds God wanted
the church to be named *Mountain Park Community Church?*
As I look back, I'd say about 100 percent.
Keep our **name** in mind as I move on to this next story.

The purchase of property on *24th Street* and *Pecos Road*
will be an account I **re-tell** forever.
After 10 years of worshipping in schools,
we were JOLTED by a notice that we had to be **out**
of our current school in nine months.
Finding *another* place to accommodate our growing church
in this short of time would be almost **impossible**.
However, if we owned land within this *nine month period*,
the school would let us stay put as we built.

We realized this need two years *earlier* and had started
the search for property then, which *revealed* many places
we **liked** but nothing we could **afford**.
We did place bids on three properties but were **out-bid**
each time. I remember *retreating* to my office
after we **lost** the bid on that third property.
It was listed for $1.5 million and we bid $1.4 million.
Someone else came in over that to **get the bid**.
I said to God in some *desperate* moments,
"I guess we're just not going to find any property. I give up."
The ironic thing about this whole process is that
even if we had **won** a bid, we wouldn't have been
able to **afford** a purchase of $1.5 million for land.
I finally **gave** the whole situation to God.

WOW! Why hadn't I done that *earlier?*

During this time, I was asked to do the funeral
                for a young couple who **lost** their baby girl at birth.
Jan, the woman who cuts my hair, *asked* me to do the funeral
                because the mother of the baby was her **best** friend.
She SHARED with me that this couple did **not** have a church
                or pastor. This wasn't the *kind* of favor I liked as a pastor,
and it turned out to be a particularly **heart-wrenching** experience.

        The first time I met David and Rebecca
                was at the funeral home. They were in such GRIEF
over losing their child it was *overwhelming.*
        I was so **broken** personally by their grief I didn't know
fully how to COMFORT them. I simply asked God to
                give me words of HOPE for their future.

Apparently I was able to SERVE as some source of *comfort* to them,
                and David and I became good friends.
        He and Rebecca began to attend MPCC *sporadically,*
                but David and I met *regularly* once a month for lunch.
He was still **coping** with the loss of his baby girl,
                and he needed that time to just SHARE his grief with me.

Hang with me as I jump one more time because there is
                a **miraculous** correlation between David and the church land.

    Doctor Farran was our family dentist
                and we had grown to **love** him over the years.
        He had shown great KINDNESS by *serving* the homeless
                people in our ministry at *Mountain Park.*
One day we told him about our need for land
                and that we had hit a *dead end* in our search.
        Dr. Farran directed me to a contact with one
                of the **most** influential people in Phoenix
when it came to real estate and land development.

            The fact that I **ended up** in this man's office
was one of those "what are the odds" stories,
                because as soon as I met him I knew he did NOT like pastors.
The way he talked *down* to me was as if I had NO business
                being there; however, somehow deep inside
I just knew he *held the key* to helping us.

I *sucked* it all up and let him talk, because he did PROMISE
to make some contacts and get back to me
and I **believed** him to be a man of his word.

What are the odds that just a few days later
I was having lunch with David on
one of our monthly meetings.
He was having a pretty **rough** day, and we had
just shared some *tears* as he talked about
Paige and his awful *sense of loss.*
I was thinking this might be the moment I could
ask David about **trusting** God with his life
in a *personal* way, when my cell phone rang.
I tried to ignore it but David **insisted** I answer.
It was the real estate giant I had met with.
In a *gruff* and *straight forward* voice he said,
"Robin, I've got land for you,
but you have to come right now."
His voice reflected an *'I'm in control and
you will come immediately'* attitude.
I began to understand that **everyone**
in his world JUMPS when he calls.

I knew there was NO WAY I could leave David.
He was in such **pain** and we were in the middle
of a deep conversation. In a *nervous* voice,
I told the man, "I'm sorry but I can't come right now.

His next words are UNPRINTABLE.
"You are a dumb s…!" Then he hung up.
I paused and thought, *"He's definitely through with me now
and any plans for land."*

David knew something **strange** had just happened
by the *look* on my face. He said,
"Hey, if you need to go it's okay."

"No, no! I absolutely don't need to go."
I was EMPHATIC if not down right **angry**.
There was NO WAY I was going to leave
an *opportunity* to be there for David
and a chance he might TRUST God that day,
all over a *bizarre, raging* real estate developer.

He smiled and thanked me, and then *gently* said,
"Robin I don't want to disappoint you,
but I'm not ready to trust God today.
I am open to how God is softening my heart."

Well I wasn't *disappointed*. How many times had I
spoken a MESSAGE about people being more important
than material wealth? I had to be **true** to myself,
even if it *cost* us that land.

After lunch, I **immediately** drove to this man's office,
and we had an *encounter* that is difficult to explain
or understand. The **first** thing he said to me
when I walked into his office was,
"Well, there's the dumb s---."

That *triggered* the WORST in me. I just lost it.
I told him in no *uncertain* terms there was only one
dumb s..., and it wasn't me. Then I ranted on,
"I don't care who you are, I'm not going to leave a man
who just lost his baby girl at birth,
to jump through your hoops.

Then I told him what he could DO with the land.
(Use your imagination.)
Not exactly **fitting words** from a pastor,
but as I said, before, I just LOST it.
I wasn't able to ask God for WISDOM,
but I think I understood for a short time
what **righteous** anger is all about.
I was no longer yelling - I was *shaking* all over.
All I wanted to do was get out of there.

I was almost to the door when the man yelled at me,
"Hey, stop. Did you just say you wouldn't leave
a lunch because you were with a man who had just
lost his baby girl, and you wouldn't leave him?"

"That's exactly what I said, and you just don't get it."
Then this man said in a quiet voice, "Sit down."

Since I was *shaking*, I sat down. I didn't know what to **expect** next.
His demeanor changed, and in a very PERSONAL and EMOTIONAL
voice he told me that he too, had **lost** a son

and it had nearly *destroyed* him.
He shared a bit more, then he said,
"If you have that kind of character,
not to leave lunch for a piece of property,
over a Dad with that kind of loss,
I will help you get your land."

What are the odds? He got on the phone
and set up a *meeting* with a man named, Dick Ziegman.
Dick had a **prime** piece of property,
15 acres to be exact, at *24th Street* and *Pecos.*
Care to guess what community this property
on 24th and Pecos was located in?
What are the odds? Ten years after losing a vote on
the name of the church, the property was right in
the middle of *Mountain Park Ranch* in Phoenix.
We finally had the **thrill** of our name matching our location.

I ask you again, what are the odds God had been
orchestrating this whole event since the dream?
As if all of this wasn't *amazing* enough,
the next "What are the Odds" story should
ROCK your world completely.

I didn't know it until I met him that first time
on the property at *24th St.* and *Pecos,*
but Dick Ziegman had heard me speak one time,
just one time, at *Mountain Point High School.*
We hadn't met on that day or any day since.
He recognized me **immediately** and told me an *unbelievable* story.
Even though he and his wife, Mary, were Catholics,
they had attended our church one time because of a
special invitation. During the service,
Dick leaned over and whispered to Mary,
"I would like to help this young man get land someday,
because he is helping so many young couples find God."

Now that day had **arrived**. He offered us the prime
15 acres of land for $500,000, **interest free.**
We could pay it off in ANY way we chose.
No *contracts*, no *loop-holes.*
He even **apologized** that he wasn't gifting us the land,

but he had PROMISED his church he
would build **one more** orphanage in Haiti.
What are the odds Dick had previously
been offered $1.8 million for the same land
from a large grocery chain.
He *turned it down* when he heard WE were
looking for land from the land developer
who **doesn't** like pastors. WOW!

Dick asked for a $100 check and a memo.
I gave him a $100 personal check and I said,
"Dick, I don't write memos."
We both laughed, as MPCC became the official
landowner of 15 acres on *24th Street* and *Pecos.*

What are the odds?
One service, one message, one moment, one phrase,
"I want to help this young man get land someday."
One AMAZING God. What are the odds?

This wasn't the **last** time Dick and I would be together.
He and his wife Mary were at the *ground breaking* service,
and after that, *once every year* they attended
a service at our church.
I asked Dick if I could **attend** with him at **his** church,
and he even asked his parish priest at
the *Holy Spirit Catholic Church* in Tempe, Arizona,
to allow me to have **communion** with them,
so he could serve me.
God was still at work in this relationship.

What are the odds? His church had NEVER before
had open communion. But beginning the Sunday I attended,
his priest got up and announced "OPEN COMMUNION"
that day and for EVERY Sunday to come.
Dick and I *shared* a warm friendship, and best of all,
we now could *share* our **faith**.

What are the odds God gave Susan Turner
the right name of the church in a dream?
What are the odds God planned for just the
right land, in just the *right place*, at just the *right time*.

What are the odds God would show us
that people are always **more** important than things?
What are the odds God would touch lives like
David and Rebecca and this real estate giant through all of this?
What are the odds, God is doing something
special in your life right NOW?

I'd say, about 100 percent.

I Missed the Wedding

I couldn't believe it! I FORGOT the wedding.
Forgetting a wedding might not be the **worst** thing
that could happen in your life, but as the *officiating* pastor,
it was a BIG DEAL. Every time I tell this story, people **gasp** and say,
"You were to perform the ceremony and you just didn't show?"

The answer will be the **same** the rest of my life,
"Yes! I totally did not show up."
I still can't believe it, I *simply* forgot.
To this day, I feel totally **embarrassed** when I tell the story.
It reminds me of when *Steve Martin* does his stand up
about the two phrases **"I forgot!"** and **"I'm sorry!"**
I felt both phrases, BIG TIME!

I first met this *young couple* through a mutual friend because
they **didn't** have a pastor to perform their ceremony.
She *taught* at a local elementary school and one of her
fellow teacher friends went to *Mountain Park Church*
and recommended me. In *addition* to the ceremony,
I do a few COUNSELING sessions with each wedding couple,
and I always **enjoy** walking them through some
role expectations and a short personality inventory,
so they can better UNDERSTAND each other.
Because of my *own devotion* to Christ,
I also make it a practice to **share** my personal story of
finding Christ and how a person can make that decision.
I think emphasizing the SPIRITUAL side of married life
is as **important** as all the other planning
that goes into a wedding and a marriage.

When this *young couple* met with me, I did ALL of the above.
When I SHARED how a person could become a *Christian*,
the young woman was **very open**
and asked me several PENETRATING questions.

"How can I know God is real and loves me?
How can I know God is concerned about my life?" She asked.

I told her, "God loves us so much he gave Christ,
His only son, to die in our place for our sins."

"But how can I know that for myself in a personal way?" she asked.

I told her "You can ask God to reveal Himself to you
through your thoughts, an impression in your mind
or spirit or ask Him to speak to you."

She responded, as many others have,
"How will I know God is speaking to me?"

"You will just know," I said.
"You will sense God saying something to you,
but it probably won't be audible.
It will be like knowing something within you,
maybe even through a dream.
It will seem so real that you might find yourself
telling others, 'God spoke to me!'
Most people won't understand how you
know God is communicating to you.
But you will know it in your heart because
you have already asked God to let you know
He cares for you and loves you."

Those were the *last words* I spoke to this sweet young woman
in that *final* counseling session.
I remember **hugging** her and telling her
she could **call** me if God spoke to her.
The wedding was a few *weeks* away,
but as I wouldn't be there for a rehearsal,
I **assured** both of them that I would BE
at the wedding about an **hour** early.
So what are the odds that I, the pastor,
for this **big event,** would FORGET something that important,

something that was on my **calendar?**
In my case, the odds were 100 percent on that day!

I had performed almost **100** weddings that past year,
and I had come CLOSE to **forgetting** one of them.
Because this close call had **scared** me so badly,
I put together a *reminder system*. I arranged for my assistant
to call me the **day before**, the morning of, and even to **text** me
a couple hours *before* the wedding.
Sounds **fool proof,** right? WRONG!

I was **gone** the *whole week* prior to this particular wedding
on a missions trip to Honduras, flying *back* into town Friday night
around midnight. I had talked to my assistant *earlier t*hat day
and told her to leave a **message** on my voicemail, which she did.
However, Saturday morning, the wedding day,
started with **distractions** that didn't let up,
and with someone like me who lives in the *world of ADHD*
(Attention Deficit Hyperactive Disorder),
distractions can often be **disastrous.**

Having **not** seen me for a week,
my young children were **waiting** for me when I got up.
Two of them told me they had ball games that day,
and I was instantly *off* and *running,* but **without** my cell phone!
I was having such a GREAT time with my children,
I didn't even **remember** to **check** my messages before I left.
I got home around 3:00 pm and *quickly* got caught up
in an exciting ballgame on TV - still **not remembering**
to check voicemail, a BIG mistake.
The wedding was at 4:00 p.m., and I got the **panic call** at 4:15 p.m.
At this point, there was NO WAY I could make the wedding,
the site was almost **45 minutes** away.

There were a **few** scenarios that could have SAVED me,
but they *didn't* happen. For example, Jeff, my youth pastor,
got a call at the church asking "Is Pastor Wood running late?"
He quickly responded with, "Don't worry. Robin wouldn't forget.
He probably is just running late!" He later told me he thought
of giving me a *quick* call but he was too **pressed** for time himself.
I was to later hear from others with a *similar* explanation,
but the *bottom line* was: I MISSED the wedding.

There were probably **300** people in attendance,
and word began to *spread* that the pastor **didn't** show.
What are the odds there would be pastor in the audience?
He wasn't **supposed** to be there, he just *happened* to be
attending with a friend of the groom. That pastor SAVED the day!

So back to my HUMILIATION. I immediately tried
to call and **plead** for forgiveness, but of course
I couldn't **reach** the bride or groom.
I left *several* messages, **profusely** apologizing for my gaffe.
Later, when the bride *returned* from her honeymoon,
I got a voicemail from her asking to *meet* with me.
As you can imagine, I was **dreading** the meeting.
From the moment she walked into my office
I began **apologizing**,
"I am so sorry, can you ever forgive me?"

She interrupted. "Pastor Robin, stop!
I have something to tell you that you will not believe.
Do you remember when you told me
I could ask God to reveal Himself to me?"

Without **waiting** for me to answer, she continued,
"Well, I prayed the entire week before the wedding
that God would make Himself known to me.
On Thursday and Friday nights I had vivid dreams
of you not showing up at the wedding.
I ignored the dreams, thinking I was just uptight."
"I now believe God was trying to tell me to call you.
In fact on Friday I shared my dream with a friend,
and she suggested I check on you.
I ignored the specific dream God gave to me twice.
So here is the great news: I gave my life to Christ
on my wedding day because you didn't show up!
The dreams from God convinced me God cared for me
personally and that I should trust Him with my life."

She could hardly contain the **excitement** in her voice.
"Pastor, I am a Christian because you blew it!"

I asked her to come to church and *share* her story.
People were moved to *tears*. Our mutual friend, Kathy,
who had **recommended** me for the wedding came to me and said,

"I can't believe it. You are off the hook.
She became a Christian because of one of the
biggest mistakes of your life!"
Friends can have a **way with words**, can't they?
But Kathy was *crying* too.

I don't share this story to let myself **off** the hook.
The **embarrassment** I felt over that specific incident
HAUNTS me every time I accept a wedding.
In fact, I tell **every** couple I marry that if I am NOT
there an hour before the wedding,
they should **call** my cell phone or any other number
they can find to *track* me down.

I share this story only because I have become **convinced**
God will do almost **anything** to communicate
that he personally **cares** for you,
including dreams before your wedding night.
God can even use our **biggest** mistakes and
a bride's **worst** nightmare to show Himself to be FAITHFUL.

The odds are 100 percent that God will do something.

The Phone Number

Y ou know you are in a **dangerous** ministry
when the people you are CARING for are named
One Eyed Mike, Liar Jim and Mean Mike!

Mean Mike didn't like pastors, he didn't like that **I** was a pastor,
and he **particularly** didn't like that a friend and I would
pick up his girlfriend and take her to church on Sunday mornings.
He was called *Mean Mike* because he was MEAN.
He didn't like *most* people and *most* things.
Wendy was his woman, but judging by the **violent** way
he *verbally* and *physically* **abused** her,
he PROVED he certainly didn't like her, either.

Wendy had given her life to Jesus at *Mountain Park Church*,
and as she grew to **know** God and **love** herself she started
realizing *Mean Mike* was not good for her,
and she didn't HAVE to live that way *anymore*.
We would *often* talk about God's love between
the church and her small, run down apartment.

We talked about her growing **strong** enough
to get out of this **violent** relationship.
Even though they *weren't* married,
at some level she considered him her SECURITY.
With time, however, Wendy began to *realize*
Jesus was her ONLY security.
She also *realized* that with **help** from Him
and the **support** from people at *Mountain Park Church*
she could break FREE of *Mean Mike*.

One Saturday afternoon Wendy called.
"It's time for me to leave and I'm scared to death."
"Is it OK for me to find a shelter for you?" I asked her.

It's a **good** thing she said "YES," because
I didn't know what I'd do with her if she said "NO."

Finding a shelter for an *abused* woman
was a new *experience* for me. I had *numbers* and *numbers*,
but I found NO shelter with an opening.
The answer at each was the **same**,
"Sorry, we have no vacant beds tonight."

Wendy had called me from a pay phone
in *Peoria*, a suburb of Phoenix.
She gave me the address and went on to tell me,
"I left everything. All I have is my purse
and the clothes on my back."

I told her, "Don't worry.
We'll go back tomorrow and get your things."
I don't know who I was **kidding**.
From what I knew of *Mean Mike*,
I wouldn't have gone back there if I'd been **paid**.

I was still dialing, **desperately** seeking a place for Wendy
to stay, when I spotted her on the corner at that moment.
A **miracle** began to unfold. I FOUND a shelter that
had a bed and they would *clear* Wendy over the phone.

She was *shaking* like a leaf by the time I got there,
standing on a corner, *unprotected* in a *not-so-great* neighborhood.
Then she told me, "Word is out, I'm leaving Mike."
To be honest, I was *shaking* a little myself.

I **quickly** hustled her into the car, but we couldn't drive far.
For some reason my cell phone would **only** work
in that ONE spot, and that spot was way *too* close
to *Mean Mike's* apartment for my comfort.

Wendy's conversation with the admittance staff person
was going *on* and *on*. She had to declare herself **drug free**.
I remember breaking into a *cold sweat* as I waited
for what seemed like an **endless** conversation to end.

Actually, it was probably only about *30 minutes*.
Finally, she was *cleared*. I got back on the phone
to receive secret instructions on how to get to the shelter
and we were on our way — AT LAST.

She looked at me and said,
"You are doing what Jesus would do, right?"
She was *nervous* and needed some *affirmation* from me.
"Well," I replied, "I am sure trying to listen to His voice.
And, Wendy, you listened to Him tonight
and you are doing a courageous thing.
You are leaving a bad life to have the
possibility of a totally new life. I am so proud of you!"

As I drove to the shelter I felt God's presence
The shelter itself was a complete **surprise**.
We drove through *two* steel fences, and there in the midst
of the city was a **beautiful** campus provided for abused women.
I introduced myself and Wendy to the head of the staff
before turning her over to three *wonderful* women.
Immediately, they made her feel LOVED and ACCEPTED.
She was given a beautiful room with **clean sheets** and **towels**.
Maybe a *first-ever* for her.

"They are so soft," she said as she buried her face in the towels.
She began to cry, then said. "Thank you for saving my life,"

I asked the leader of the shelter for her phone number.
I explained the people at *Mountain Park Church*
would like to make a FINANCIAL donation
and that I would get back in touch with her on Monday.

She walked me to my car. I reached inside
for the yellow pad where I had **written** the
shelter's number that afternoon.
Then I asked her for the number she
wanted me to call on Monday.

As she gave me her *personal* number for Monday's call,
I looked at my sheet and said, "I already have that number,
it's the one I called tonight to get Wendy in this shelter."
"No," she insisted, "You couldn't have called that number
because that number doesn't ring in here.

I'm giving you my personal number
that doesn't ring into the shelter."
"No look," as I pointed to the number written on the yellow sheet.
"It's the only number I have for this shelter and I called it tonight."

Then I *pulled out* my cell phone
and the same number was on my phone.

She *looked* down at the sheet in my hand,
looked at my cell phone, and *pointed* to the number.
She was STUNNED! "Is that the only number you have
for this shelter? Is that the number you called today?" she asked.
She continued, "That is my personal number. It doesn't ring
at the shelter, it rings at my home, 10 miles from here!"

We came to the same conclusion almost *simultaneously:*
We had just witnessed a **miracle**!

She said, "It wouldn't have mattered what the number was.
I think God would have put any number you dialed
through to this shelter just to save Wendy's life."
I had dialed her personal number and the phone rang to the shelter.

What are the odds? With God, 100 percent!

Don't Worry,
Stay Right Where You Are!

As I look back on the *events* that placed me just **two** blocks from the *Twin Towers* on September 11, I can't even BEGIN to figure the odds of me being there. Only God knows.

The events that put me in New York on 9-11 started several years before, on my **first** mission trip to Honduras, this is where *Paul Keeler* and I bonded for life.

Later, Paul and I decided to go *back* to Honduras on another mission trip in February 2001.

Paul was now vice-president of *Hilton's* food and beverage division and he wanted to treat me (his pastor) to a FUN vacation.

As we stood in the small village of *Cachias*, he asked, "Of any place in the world, where would you like to go? Being in Honduras with you has changed my life and I want to take you anywhere you want to go on vacation."

I didn't hesitate. "I've always wanted to go to the US Open tennis championship, which will be in New York in September."

The fact that I chose somewhere in the **United States** seemed to have SURPRISED him. After all, he had offered anywhere in the world.

"Is that really where you want to go?" he asked.

"Yep, that's exactly it."

Paul made ALL the arrangements, and in September my wife and I

flew with Paul and his wife, Judy, to New York City.
We stayed at *The Embassy Suites* in Battery Park,
approximately **two** blocks from the *World Trade Center*.

What a FUN time! As you may have assumed,
I am an AVID tennis fan, and this was a tennis match
that would make **history**: two African American sisters
playing each other in the **finals** of the *US Open*,
Venus and *Serena Williams*.
Now there are some ODDS to consider.

We had tickets for the Finals weekend, but the *Open* had
changed venues for the women's finals.
If we wanted to be there, we were going to have to **scalp**
tickets for Saturday night. Guess who was chosen to do that
for the four of us? Of course ME.

I got them at a GREAT price and even though they were
on the very **top** row of the 20,000-seat *Arthur Ashe* stadium,
it barely detracted from the *excitement*.
In two **thrilling** sets, the younger sister Serena took the **title**.
In the next day of the *Open*, the *feisty* Aussie, Lleyton Hewitt,
took Pete Sampras out in **three** straight sets.
What a GREAT tennis weekend.

On Monday, Paul and Judy flew back to Phoenix,
and we *remained* in New York Tuesday and Wednesday
to do some *shopping* and see a couple of shows on *Broadway*.
Paul had gotten us a **great** corner suite on the 12th floor
with a beautiful glass view of the *Statue of Liberty*
and the *World Trade Center* towers.

I was up early Tuesday morning and had gone for a workout
in the hotel gym. At 9:00 a.m. I was back in my room showering
when there was a BLAST so **powerful** I was almost knocked
out of the shower. I came out of the bathroom and Carma
had turned on the TV, as the announcer said a small plane
had HIT the north tower. We then pulled back the curtains
of our room and we could **see** the tower where the plane hit
and the **massive** fire starting. We stared in DISBELIEF.

I *quickly* dressed, took the elevator downstairs,
and walked outside to the corner. I spotted a police officer

and asked, "What's happening?" He looked back at me
with a **blank** look and didn't seem to know any more than I did.
I stood there for about 15 minutes, *gawking* with everyone else.
The atmosphere around me *changed*, however,
as people in the **top** of the tower started JUMPING
to their death right in front of our eyes.
I have **no** words to describe the HORROR of what we were witnessing.
I felt like I was going to THROW UP.

The officer asked me to *escort* two women back
to the hotel and to also *inform* another officer at the corner
that **no one** was to be allowed any **closer** to the north tower.
I said a *prayer* with the women and took them back to the hotel.
As for myself, I was in a mild **state of shock**.
Too **numb** to keep praying, I walked to the corner to
deliver the message to the officer.

In the lobby I **ran** into *Steve*, the hotel manager.
Paul had introduced us the day before, telling him,
"Watch out for my pastor."

The **first** thing Steve said to me was,
"Don't worry, everything is going to be OK.
Don't panic, stay right where you are."
The hotel must have DRILLED those phrases
into **all** their personnel because those words
became a **mantra**, blaring out from the intercom
every few minutes into EVERY room in the hotel.

To use an old phrase, Steve was the **epitome** of *cool, calm* and *collected*.
Taking me by the elbow, he led me to the breakfast bar
and calmly said, "Robin, you need breakfast."
Despite ALL I had seen, he **succeeded** in calming me.
Looking back, I was probably in **deeper** shock
than I thought at the time. I *calmly* ordered an omelet
and hash browns to take to the room.

Before he moved on to calm someone else, Steve said,
"I think people are panicking and believing false reports.
I don't believe planes are hitting other buildings or the Pentagon."

I hadn't heard these reports, so I just went along with his reasoning.
After all, I realized, **rumors** and **exaggerations** do go

hand in hand with catastrophes.

I told the cook who was making my omelet,
    "Hold it for me, I'll be right back," and hurried over to a large
TV screen about 50 feet away. I was OVERWHELMED at what I saw.
        A **huge** jetliner was flying INTO the south tower!
    We weren't hearing **rumors**…this was PROOF.

I remember going back to Steve.
        "This is happening, Steve! Jets are flying into other buildings.
One just flew into the south tower!"
        The funny thing is I **can't** remember how Steve reacted,
but I **do** know my reaction was totally *out of character* for me.
        I'm the guy who wants to FIX everything and everybody,
    but I *calmly* went back, got my tray to take up to my room,
            and then looked around for grape jelly for myself
    and cranberry juice for Carma.

I walked into our room with the breakfast tray.
            Carma yelled at me, a look of **disbelief** on her face.
    "Are you crazy? I'm not going to eat. Let's get out of here!"

        Looking back, shock can do **awful** things to the *reasoning*
part of the mind, and if I never *believed* it before, I do **now**.

    She had no sooner gotten those words out,
before the intercom *blared* again,
        "Don't worry, everything is going to be OK.
    Don't panic, stay right where you are."

All of a sudden we felt **another** earthquake jolt
        and our TV went blank. Finally, a voice came over the intercom:
"We need to evacuate the hotel." There were other instructions,
        but we were OUT OF THERE, and we left **everything** behind.

We **rushed** down the stairs and out of the building.
        The air was filled with *white dust,* which settled all over us,
in our nose and throat. We *coughed* and *choked* as we
        blindly followed the crowd. We ended up at a small park
    by the *Hudson River.*

Sure enough, there was an officer there REPEATING
        those **same** old phrases, "Don't worry…" I tuned out the rest of it.
Something inside me **snapped** and I *finally* came to my senses.

What we were hearing was NOT the truth,
even if it was being said by a *police officer*.
We needed to get OUT of that area as **fast** as we could.

I asked the officer, "Which way is north?"
He directed us to a high school where a *triage* was being set up,
but when we found the *main* route north we just kept **going**.

After we had gone about five or six blocks we were able
to get a cell phone call through to Carma's mother.
We had just finished talking to her when
I heard the **loudest** rumble I have ever heard in my LIFE.
The north tower was **coming down right before our eyes**,
and we were no more than *10 blocks* away.

We stood *frozen*, watching in what seemed to be *slow motion*
as the building came down. It looked like the **atomic bomb explosions**
we had watched on TV, except this was VERY REAL.

Debris came at us like a *tidal wave*. **Adrenalin** gave extra *strength*
and we began to run away from the debris, with fear the debris
could **engulf** us at any minute is what kept us moving.
At the end of five blocks we could *barely* get our breath.
We stopped and looked back. I was **shocked**,
I saw total DESTRUCTION.

We kept walking for about *three and a half hours*.
There was a crowd of us and I don't know if most of us knew
where we were going, but we all knew we **had** to get away.
The mood was one of *fear* and *grief, anger* and *awful fatigue*.

I remember raising my voice and asking someone,
"Do any of you know where a Doubletree or Hilton Hotel is located?"
They yelled back, "At 53rd and Broadway."

We *kept* going until we found that corner. I *knew* if we could
get a call through to Paul, he would take CARE of us.
We *finally* got the call through and sure enough, he had **already**
made the arrangements. The first thing he said was,
"I knew you would walk to a Double Tree if you were okay.
Go to the manager's office and he will give you a key."
"It's his room, the only one available." Then he cautioned me,
"Don't ask him any questions. He doesn't have time to talk."

We *stayed* in that room for the **five** days
before we could get a flight back to Phoenix.

As I REFLECT on those five days, I **know** God had many things
to *teach* me. We had been close to one of the most
TRAUMATIC events in history, yet during those days in the hotel,
I realized we all need **stability** in our lives.
Something so *mundane* as going to the *same* coffee shop
for the *same* food everyday began to feel normal.
We were **never** going to get back to retrieve our things
from the *Embassy Suites*, but it no longer seemed to matter.
Material things **weren't** important, LIFE was.

Our hearts were **aching** for the countless people
who came through the hotel looking for *lost* loved ones.
Our floor housed the canine dogs and personnel
who searched the rubble. We particularly tried to ENCOURAGE
and PRAY with those people.

I did a good deal of *soul searching* during those five days.
One thing became VERY clear: We should **not** have put
our faith in **false** phrases. We should have *panicked*
and *left* the hotel **sooner** than we did.

A pilot from our church arranged for us to fly home.
We arrived in Phoenix on Sunday morning, September 16th,
just in time to make the first service at church.
Care to guess what my *message* was about that morning?
What are the odds? "Don't worry, everything is going to be OKAY.
Don't panic, stay right where you are."

I gave this simple message to our people:
"We often buy into false statements.
I had heard trusted people say over 20 times on 9-11,
'Don't worry, everything is going to be OKAY, don't panic,
stay right where you are!'
All four statements were false that day and I fear
many of us are believing these false statements
in our spiritual lives. We need to worry when we've lost our way.
Today would be a great day to say,
'I don't need to stay where I am.'
If I am caught in an addiction, living in a broken marriage,
putting my hope in material things, or

living without Christ at the center of my life,
I need to panic and turn to God. Today is the day to say,
'Everything is not okay in my life. I need to change.

We had *hundreds* of decisions that day and our church
truly changed out of this experience.

So what are the odds God wants us to simply confess
to him that *"Everything is **not** OKAY."*

The odds are 100 percent.

Jay and the TV

I had been a **devoted** follower of Jesus
for only a few years when I had my
FIRST "What are the Odds" experience.
I was in my early twenties and was always **excited**
to tell someone how Jesus had *changed* my life.
I was serving as youth pastor at a church in
Eaton, Indiana under senior pastor Ken Mishler.
He is still a SPIRITUAL hero to me.
Ken **strongly** believed God could do ANYTHING.
He preached that message and definitely **lived** what he preached.
As crazy as this sounds, one day Ken actually
prayed his *Volkswagen* would be **healed**.
I'll leave you guessing at how God *answered*
that prayer, but will say that an occasional
"NO" from God never *dampened* his faith.

Pastor Mishler believed in praying for **specifics**,
whether praying for *people* or *situations*.
In my **excitement** to win others to Jesus
I decided I would be very *specific* in my prayers.
I made a list of all the people in my sphere of
influence that I could personally talk to about the gospel.
Then I began to *specifically* pray for God to open
the door of OPPORTUNITY for me to talk to each of them.

Jay Ullom was one of these people on my list.
His wife, Rita had already *opened* her heart
to Jesus, and their children were in the
Eaton children's choir I directed.

The only time Jay ever **entered** the church door
was when his children were performing,
or at *Easter* or *Christmas Eve.*
Please don't think I am being **critical**
of Jay's limited attendance,
I simply wanted MORE for him.
I wanted Jay to have a **real** relationship with Christ.

I **often** stopped by the Ullom home, as I genuinely liked to
hang out with Jay and we were *building* a friendship.
We both LOVED basketball; he was a big *Indiana University*
fan and a **devoted** Coach Bobby Knight follower.
The biggest game of every year was *Indiana* versus *Purdue.*

Knowing Jay had a **large** new TV, I asked if I could
come by and *watch* the game with him.
As I started for Jay's house that evening,
I was **overwhelmed** with a *strong* sense that God
wanted me to WITNESS to Jay that night.
I knew I couldn't just **start** talking about my faith
during the game, so I asked God,
"Give me a sign if you want me to share my faith with
Jay tonight. Make it very clear to me if this is the night."

I *prayed* out loud in my car all the way to
the house with a sense of **urgency**.
I arrived just at the tip off. The TV was *blaring,*
the kids were *running* all over the place, and soon
we were caught up in the **excitement** of the game.
Halftime came and went as we got some
junk food and talked about the first half.
Indiana was up by two and they were playing well.
To be honest, I almost **forgot** the *urgency* and feeling
I had spent so much time *praying* about on my way over.

It was when Jay went to the back bedroom to
put the kids to bed that I *remembered* what God
had put on my heart, and I whispered,
"God please give me a sign.
I need it to be an obvious sign if this is the night."

Jay returned and the second half began.
I was feeling pretty **tense** thinking about sharing
my FAITH with Jay, when suddenly the TV screen
went *totally* blank. Jay **rushed** out to check the breaker.
He even went outside to the main box
to see if the circuit could be out, but **no** luck.
The TV was NOT going to come back on.

I remember thinking, "*God is this the sign?*"
I must have been waiting for God to
HIT me over the head with a baseball bat.
We sat there in silence for a few minutes,
and Jay's **frustration** was mounting.
Finally I started to speak, and rather *nervously* I might add.
"Jay, I don't know how to say this,
but I've been praying since I left home tonight.
Can I tell you what I've been praying about?"
He kindly said, "Yes."

"I asked God to give me a sign if He wanted
me to share my faith with you."

Jay became **silent** for a bit. I wasn't sure how
he was *receiving* all this, but I plunged ahead.
"Jay, I think the TV outage is from God. Can I tell you
my personal story how God has changed my life?"

A spirit of *openness* and *graciousness* came over Jay.
His response "Yes, you can share," was all I needed.
I think we both were feeling that this
was a **magical** moment from God.

I told him how God had not only **forgiven** my sins,
but that God had been changing some pretty *bad habits*
in my life. We both sensed God's *presence* and when I got **brave**
enough to ask him if he wanted to ask Jesus into his life,
I shouldn't have been so **surprised** at his quick response.
He almost shouted one simple word, "Yes!"

What are the odds God wants us to pray
specifically for **special** people in our sphere of influence?
And what are the odds that it is **okay** to ask for a "SIGN"
if we care about someone SPIRITUALLY?

I think the odds are 100 percent.

Leave it up to God to come through with the *sign.*

What do you have to lose?

Why not take the risk?

Luca Vida

What a **fantastic** summer vacation!
I was *seeing* and *experiencing* everything we had planned for Europe:
a **great** tennis tournament at *Wimbledon* in England,
a tour of *castles* in France, tennis played on Germany's *red clay*,
plus the **rush** of hang gliding from a *14,000 foot* mountain in Germany.

Then, in Switzerland, I had what I call a SERENDIPITY Moment…
a completely **unplanned** experience.
I was going to get to **ski** the world-renowned *Matterhorn* glacier.

Before I tell you of the *actual* skiing,
let me tell you how really CHEAP I can be at times.
Of course I had to *rent* the skis, but I didn't want to
spend money to rent ski clothing.
I decided my cuffed dress *pants* and golf *shirt* would work just **fine**.
"Besides," I thought to myself, *"I'm not going to see anyone
I know, the day is warm, so I don't need ski clothes."*

I was *thoroughly* enjoying myself until I caught a ride up the lift
with a young, *buff-looking* skier, dressed in the LATEST ski outfit.
There was an **air** about him that said,
"I'm not all looks, I'm a darned good skier."
I **sheepishly** looked down at my cuffed dress pants and told myself,
*"Don't talk, look straight ahead, and above all,
no personal conversation."*
But all that **changed** when he turned to me and said,
"I'm Luca Vida, what's your name?"
"Robin," I responded. "Where are you from?" he asked.

"Phoenix, Arizona!" I tried to *avoid* anything further by looking away and not **asking** any questions back.

We were **finally** at the top.
"On my way, and no more Luca Vida," I told myself.
However, about thirty minutes later, I was *back* at the bottom and getting on the same lift.
You guessed it…**Luca Vida** was in line with me again.

He asked MORE questions of me,
as I broke my *"no conversation"* rule.
I told him I was a pastor, and he looked
right at me and said, "I am a new Christian!"
WOW! What are the odds?
What a **great** moment, as we were towed up the hill.

He was so hungry in his *new* faith he began
to **bombard** me with *questions*, and I answered
as many as I could in **rapid** fire.

When we got to the top of the hill, I asked him
"Can I ski with you?" I will **never** forget
his response: "Don't think you can!"
"What?" I was indignant. "You don't think I can?"

He repeated, "Don't think you can! I am the number one
speed skier on the Swiss Olympic Team. I am a
down hill, Super G specialist and was thinking
about going down at about 100 miles an hour."

He wasn't **bragging**…just stating a FACT.
I looked at him, *laughed*, and said, "I don't think I can."

There was a definite HUMILITY in my voice.
He pointed to my clothes and asked,
"New style in the United States?"
I had to **again** laugh at myself.
"No, too cheap to rent the right clothes."

Here I was on the **top** of the *Matterhorn* with
the number **one** skier on the *Swiss Olympic team*,
and I still had the AUDACITY to ask again,
"Can I come over and do the slalom with you?"
To my *amazement* he said "Yes", and we skied over to the slalom.

He got on the **intercom** and said to his coach:
> "I have a Christian pastor from the United States
who wants to try the slalom!"

I heard, "Send him down." I made about four gates
and then I was **out-of-control**. From the bottom
> I watched Luca ski the slalom run PERFECTLY.

When he got to the bottom, I asked him, "What did I do wrong?"
> "Go ask the coach for some teeps," he said in his accent.
I couldn't **understand** him until he finally
> *spelled* out for me "T-I-P-S."
> "Oh I get it, TIPS!" as I went over to his coach.

And again, to my **amazement,** the coach was *willing* to help me.
"You are flailing away with your arms, making motions out to the side."
> Sarcastically, he said, "Not much hope for you!"
But then he touched me on the shoulder and said,
> "Try again. Stay tucked and trust yourself."

Well, to make a long story short, the coach *stayed*
> with me for *four* more tries and I **finally** got it.
There I was in my dress *pants* and golf *shirt*,
> and the whole *Swiss Olympic Ski team*
> **stood** and **applauded** me.

Luca and I spent **a lot** of time *talking* that day.
> He was coming back to skiing from
a very **serious** injury. I sensed he needed
> ENCOURAGEMENT as to whether he could make it.
I told him I would *pray* for him daily.
> I encouraged him, "Since you are a new Christian,
do it for God this time. Keep telling yourself...
> 'I CAN DO IT!' You can do it, Luca. I know you can."

We *exchanged* e-mail addresses, and we **actually** stayed
> in touch throughout the *Winter Olympics* in Utah.
Although he didn't win ANY medals,
> he placed in the **top 15** in the world.

I received an e-mail from him within
> two weeks after leaving Europe that said,
*"Robin, you changed my life! I now know God
> brought you in my life to convince me that I can do it."*

WOW! What are the odds? Surely someone *else* had said
those same words "You can do it," to him before.
I have come to BELIEVE it was a "What are the Odds" moment!

We **never** know when we are going to be
used by God, even in *ridiculous* clothing.
What are the odds God wants to use you
and your words to *encourage* someone?

With God...100 percent!

John Younkins, My Friend

In the beginning days of *Mountain Park Community Church*
we explored a variety of ways of **reaching out** to
the *Mountain Park Foothills* community.
Our **main** focus was to simply meet people.

I have always *believed* my part is to *hang out* with people
who have **never** known a loving God, and to build *relationships*
with those who have **never** had a trusted Christian friend.
My GREATEST memories of those early days of the church
come from the times I made those *personal* efforts.
That's why I was *off and running* when my family and I moved to
our new home in a new development called *Mountain Side*.

I was **determined** to knock on every door in my large
neighborhood of over **2000** homes. My **main** motive was
to be a *good* neighbor and to be ACCEPTED as a friend.

As I knocked on doors, I got *acquainted* by first introducing myself,
and then asking for their help in a simple survey.
I also left a GIFT at each household, an album *recorded* by my wife Carma.
I wanted them to experience the *joy* and *energy* of the kind of music
we were going to use at the new church.
I was **hoping** they would visit us because of the music,
as music does have a way of *breaking down barriers*.

I will never forget the **first** person I met. His name was *John Younkins*.
He, his wife Annette, and their three BEAUTIFUL children
lived a couple of blocks from our home.

On our first meeting John wasn't **too** friendly.
I think I can say that he barely **talked** to me.
However, I sensed a TENDER SPIRIT hidden beneath
that **hard** exterior and I wanted to be his friend.

I gave him one of Carma's albums and invited him
and his family to church. He and Annette **did** attend —
SPORADICALLY — but the kids attended
the *Youth Hot Church* on a regular basis.

After about *two years*, John asked me for a second album
because the kids had totally worn out the first one.
He said, "It's our family's favorite album."

Over the years, I CONTINUED to try and be friendly
to John and his family, but his guard was **always** up.
I always passed his house on my way home on 42nd St.,
and sometimes I stopped to say "HI"
if I saw him working in his yard.

I'm sure he thought I was too PERSISTENT,
but I felt a need to get to know him.
I often *wondered* if he would **ever** give his heart to Christ.
There was no **visible** sign of that happening
during the first 13 years I knew him.

In the summer of 2001, I began to see John
at church EVERY Sunday. This was **very** strange.
He came alone, and he had **never** before attended *regularly*.
He ALWAYS sat in an area where he wasn't *easily* noticed,
and after church he NEVER lingered
to say more than a short greeting.

This went on for **several** Sundays. Finally, I *bluntly* asked him,
"Why are you coming to church each week"?
Tears began to form in his eyes.
"I'm losing my marriage," he replied.
"Come see me," I told him. "I want to be there for you."

"I will," he promised, but he NEVER came.
This went on for the remaining Sundays of the summer.
I extended the invitation, he **promised** to come,
and NOTHING changed.

Finally, in October I noticed my assistant
had scheduled John to see me. I was **thrilled** that he
mustered up enough COURAGE to come and talk to me.

He walked in, and after an emotional conversation about his
pending divorce, he asked me, "How do I become a Christian?"
WOW! After all those years of my trying to
build a *friendship* and *praying* for him,
he is **finally** asking me how to become a Christian.

I explained the Gospel to him in a *simple* way, and right there
in my office John *prayed* and *received* Christ.
With tears streaming down both our faces,
I then *prayed* for John. After the prayer, I felt **compelled**
to do something I hadn't done in years.
I reached for a blank piece of paper
and a calendar sitting on my desk.

I told John, "I want you to always remember your
spiritual birthday. I'm going to write it down.
I used to do this all the time when someone
came to Christ, but I've gotten out of practice."

As I looked at my calendar, I wrote down the date,
October 18, 2001. I could hardly **believe** it.
"John you won't believe what I am going to tell you.
What are the odds? We held our first public worship service
at Mountain Park Community Church on October 18, 1987.
Fourteen years later, to the day, on October 18, 2001,
John, you give your life to Christ!
What are the odds?"

What are the odds the **first** person
in my neighborhood that I had invited to
the **first** service in our church would be *giving*
his heart to Christ exactly 14 years later?
For years I had thought John would be one of the
most *unlikely* candidates to come to Christ.
What are the odds?
I think the odds might be 100 percent.

Then, in 2005 there came a **second part** to this story:

I had been invited *back* to Phoenix to perform a wedding.
I hardly knew the couple, but they had contacted me
                through my son, *Brady*. At the rehearsal I had the bride
and groom *introduce* their family and friends
                and tell the role each were *filling* for the wedding.

When they introduced the *maid of honor,*
                I didn't catch her last name, but she looked right at me
and asked, "Do you remember me?" "You look familiar," I answered,
                "but sorry, I can't remember how I know you."
"I'm John Younkin's daughter. I know every word on Carma's album."

                I immediately asked, "How is your dad?"
        "You led my Dad to Christ, and he's changed so much,"
                        she said. "He's a different man."
        She continued, "Because there has been such
                a huge change in my Dad's life
since he came to Christ, I am now a Christian too!"
                She then threw her arms around me and tightly hugged me.
        "My father is wanting to get in touch with you.
                He said you helped him through his divorce, and he
        wants to be there for you in the loss of your marriage."

                What are the odds a man that I
unsuccessfully tried for years to *befriend*
                would now become a friend and a GREAT source
        of ENCOURAGEMENT to me?
                As always, when God is in it,
        the odds are 100 percent.

It's Not Who You Know

How many times have you *heard* the phrase,
"It's who you know in this life that matters?"
It's not WHAT you know, but WHO you know.
Well, I have learned another *lesson* and another *phrase*
that I'll tell you, after this "What are the Odds" story.

About 7 years ago, I had an *unusual* experience
that reminded me of my **shadow** side.
This is not one of my *darkest* parts, but one
that I *continually* have to work on personally.
I am a **high-energy** person with very **little** patience.
I also am the type of person that processes thoughts out LOUD.
Meaning, I usually only **open** my mouth long enough
to *exchange feet*. I say things that I don't FULLY mean literally.

With that information, here's the story and experience.
I was up early at 5 a.m. to catch a flight from Phoenix
to Columbus, Ohio to speak for a fairly large church.
I was on my way to the airport at about 6 a.m.
when I noticed that my flight with *Southwest*
had **3** other stops before my arrival in Columbus
(I've learned *Southwest* will stop **anywhere** someone's
waving a white handkerchief, saying "Pick me up!")
I wondered **why** I was on this flight since there are
at least three **non-stop** flights every day to Columbus.
So I picked up my cell phone to call my assistant.
She answered, and I asked about the connections.
She had only been working for me a short time
so when she proudly said, "Robin, I saved $60 on this flight."

I replied, "I don't do connections for that small of savings."
Then in a frustrated voice, (my **shadow side**) I said,
"I don't want to be on this flight!"
I continued processing out loud,
"I can't believe I'm on this flight, I don't want to be on this flight."
But hey, I was on my way to the airport,
no turning back now. My final words,
"I don't do connections unless I have to, goodbye!"
I turned into long-term parking and
dragged my bags with me on the shuttle.
I took my golf clubs, just in case my friend
in Columbus was able to **sneak** us on at the
Nicklaus Course where they play the Memorial.
For those of you who know me,
my face tends to sweat **profusely** when
my *adrenaline* is up and I'm running just a little late.
So I'm *dragging* three bags and a towel.
If you know me, you're *smiling*.

I went in the terminal to check in.
After **twenty** minutes of waiting, TOO long for me,
I was at the counter. I handed my license to the young woman
behind the counter and she punched a few keys on
the computer and then looked up at me and announced,
"Mr. Wood, you've been cancelled from this flight."
"No, that's impossible," I responded.
"I just talked to my assistant and she
gave me the confirmation number."

She then said, "You were cancelled about 15 minutes ago."
I got on my cell phone and my assistant picked up.
I **began** to explain the situation when my assistant said,
"You just told me you didn't want to be on this flight."

I couldn't BELIEVE what I was hearing.
"I didn't say take me off the flight and you knew
I was on my way to the airport!"

She responded, "But you said, 'I don't want to be on this flight.'"

My **shadow side** was about ready to EXPLODE. I hung up.

I turned to the woman behind the counter and said,

"I really need to be on this flight,
my assistant misunderstood me."
I continued to talk *nervously*, "I have to be on this flight."
She punched a number of keys, looked up at me,
and announced, "I can get you back on for $819."

"I can't do that," I pleaded with her.
Then I saw a tag on her uniform that made me
unbearably nervous. The tag said, TRAINEE.
I've traveled enough to know that a trainee has NO power
to change **anything**. I took my voice UP a notch and said,
"I've got to talk to someone who is in charge."
"Sir, I can't do anything." She said.

Then my **shadow side** kicked into high gear.
"I need a manager or supervisor."
I was almost **shouting** by now. I caught hold of myself
and said, "Please help me, I have to be on this flight
and I can't afford to lose it here.
And I really can't pay the increase."

I kept *pleading* with her, when out of **nowhere**,
a woman who had overheard me speaking
TOO loudly came over to the computer.
Without saying *anything*, she began to punch
the letters on the computer. I started talking to her
and asking if she could *please* help me get back on the flight.
I kept saying, "I don't want to lose it,
can you help me get back on."
She paid no attention to me, but kept typing.

My heart **jumped** a beat when I saw the tag on her blouse.
It said, SUPERVISOR. However, she **wasn't** talking to me,
just typing *frantically*. I was trying to explain what happened
with my assistant and was *bumbling* all over myself
about how I couldn't afford **$819** and so on,
when she stopped and looked up at me.

One more time I said, "I can't lose it in public
and embarrass myself. I need your help."

She looked straight at me and said,
"Mr. Wood, you're back on the flight, with no increase.

I don't want you to lose it and embarrass yourself either."

I will NEVER forget her next set of words,
"Because," she said, "Pastor, we just starting
attending your church four weeks ago."

Then she smiled. "I would hate to tell your board
you lost it in the airport.
And by the way, my husband loves
your messages, and he has refused to go
to church with me our entire marriage."

What are the odds?
Of course I thanked her **profusely** and as I walked away,
I thought, **"It's not who you know in this life
that really matters, it's who knows you,
that you don't know knows you that really counts!"**

What are the odds that someone you **don't** know,
knows you, and is just waiting to see
how you will *react* under pressure?
What are the odds God wants you to
lose your shadow side, so He can use you
to *influence* someone for Him?
And what are the odds, you are always
on display with your *character* and your *words?*

I'd say about 100 percent of the time!

What a Game,
What an Ending!

What a **night**! What a **game**!
It was *Miami* vs. *Ohio State* in the
College National Championship football game.
Date: January 4, 2001.
Location: *Sun Devil Stadium* in Tempe, Arizona.

My friend Wally had gotten us the seats
and we found ourselves sitting **smack-dab**
in the middle of the *Miami Hurricane's* fan section.
Not a **great** place to be when there were only four of us
in the *whole* section who were *Ohio State Buckeyes* fans.

We didn't let that diminish our **enthusiasm** until
the *Hurricanes* started yelling their chant:
It's great...to be... a part...of a hurricane!
Especially, since they felt **compelled** to yell it *over*
and *over* and *over* again. (Ad-nausea)

In between chants we got into friendly **banter** with their fans.
Actually we were having a GREAT time with them,
friendly rivalry at its best. We expressed *admiration* for their
leading rusher, Willis McGahee, and they had some *kind* words
about the *Buckeyes'* star running back, Maurice Clarett.
Note, however, we did NOT join their chant.

What a **night**! What a **game**! What an **ending**!
The *Ohio State Buckeyes* went for one final play to tie the game.

That pass was initially ruled **incomplete**,
and then came the **late** flag!
In fact, the flag was SO late most of the
Hurricane fans were already **on** the field.
The four of us *Buckeyes* fans had *conceded* defeat
and were picking up our coats and gear,
getting ready to leave.

Suddenly, we hear over the loudspeaker,
"clear the field...clear the field! There has been a flag on the play."
Remember the famous saying, "It ain't over until it's over!"

The field was cleared and *Ohio State* was given ONE more
play in which they scored the **game-tying** touchdown
and sent the game into **overtime**.
Then the REAL excitement began.
Both teams scored in the first overtime
and then in **double** overtime *Ohio State* wins this thrilling
National Championship Game. The four of us Buckeyes fans
became a **mini-hurricane** ourselves.

This was a "What are the Odds" game all right,
and the ruling and final flag in regulation time
will probably be *contested* for years.
However, this is just **part** of the story.
To tell the rest, I need to give you some background
on my brother-in-law, Doug.

Doug is a die-hard *Buckeyes* fan. At one time he had season
tickets at the big horseshoe stadium in Columbus, Ohio.
What an OPPORTUNITY, what a **dream come true**
for a die-hard *Buckeyes* fan. He actually got to follow weekly
one of the **greatest** college football programs in the country,
and he could personally be at ALL of their home games.

However, as he later admitted to me,
that **love** of football and his **love** of the *Buckeyes*
had become a **controlling** force in his life.
If the team lost, he was **overwhelmed**
with *disappointment* and *anger*.

Meantime, back at the stadium,
I pulled out my cell phone and told our group,

"I have to call everyone we can think of that loves Ohio State."
We wanted to talk with *anyone* and *everyone*
about the game, go over **every** play and celebrate one of
the **greatest** moments in *Ohio State* football history.

"Call Doug," someone shouted. "I bet he's ecstatic."
His wife picked up the phone and said, "Hello?"

Without even *identifying* myself,
the first words out of my mouth were,
"Unbelievable! Unbelievable! What a game!"

In a very calm voice she replied, "Yeah, I guess."
"What? You can only say 'I guess?' That's all?"
It didn't take but a second to *realize*
she didn't **care** for football or *Ohio State*.
How could anyone be so **calm** after such a **great** game?

"Let me talk to Doug," I shouted.
However, when he picked up the phone
he was just as *low key* and *calm* as Stephanie.
In fact, he even seemed **despondent**.
There definitely was NO joy in his tone.

"What a game! What a game!"
I kept shouting with enthusiasm.
By now all I got from him was **silence**.

Finally, I pleaded, "Come on Doug, what's wrong?
Ohio State just won the game of the century."

"Don't tell me that. They lost," he shot back,
his voice now raised a bit.

"They didn't lose, Doug. They won the game in overtime."
Then it hit me. "Doug, did you turn off your TV
at the end of the game?"
"Yes," he said, in a dejected voice.
"Oh, no, Doug, you missed the flag in the end zone.
That's how late the flag was thrown!" I told him.

"Don't play with me, Robin. Did they win? Did they really win?"
Doug later explained to me he was so **overwhelmed**
by the loss and that he didn't want to *spiral out* in his anger over it.

He had really done the most **mature** thing for him.

So often before, he had been personally *controlled* by
the **overwhelming** disappointment of *Ohio State* losing.

He didn't want the *disappointment* and
anger to TOTALLY control his life.

I was **proud** of this part of his *decision* to turn off the T.V.

However, I had to get Doug *back* in the real world
that his *Buckeyes* had won.

"Doug, you can turn on Sports Center and find out for yourself.

They'll be showing it the rest of the night along
with that great music, da da da....da da da!

Trust me, they really won Doug!"

No point in trying to figure the odds of one of the *Buckeyes*
biggest fans turning OFF the TV too soon
on the team's best-ever **come-back** game.

And even though his reasons were *good* and *personal*,
Doug had missed the **best** part of the best game played in years.

I do, however, want you to think about the odds
in these questions: Have you **turned off** God
before the last chapter in you life has been written?

Have you made **poor** choices that make you
think you can't go on, or be FORGIVEN?

Well, I've got **good** news for you, you can hope AGAIN!

None of us have seen the FINAL chapter of our life.

What are the odds you have simply given up too **soon**
and switched the "GOD BUTTON" off?

What are the odds God still wants to give you a *second* chance,
that God's future for you is for **good** and not for **evil**?

Do you really think it's TOO late for you?

Let me remind you of one of the GREATEST stories
at the end of the Bible, a story of two **criminals**,
each *nailed* to a cross with Jesus between them.

All three were minutes away from death.

The one criminal *ridiculed* and *railed* at Jesus.

He turned off God just minutes **before** his death.

He had the same *opportunity* as the other criminal who,
with his *last* breath, turned to Jesus and said:

"Lord, remember me today when you come into your kingdom."

And with almost his *last* breath, Jesus replied,
"This day you will be with me in paradise."
What are the odds, a life can be changed in a moment?
What are the odds God would respond to you if you whispered something like "Remember me today."

I think 100 percent.

Annie's Cross Necklace

I have three children who are **extraordinary**.
They are adults now, but I've *felt* this way since the day
they were born. I can RELATE to Moses' parents.
Hebrews says, *"When Moses was born his parents saw that
he was no ordinary child."*

For all of us who have *children* let me tell you:
No child is **ordinary**. One of my *greatest* lessons
in life is to learn that *each* of my three children
are not only **different**, each is **unique**.

As a father I still LOVE to give gifts to my adult children.
I try to make each gift *fun* and *meaningful*.

I have a **great** memory of a special *Christmas gift*
I gave to Annie, my youngest, when she was
a SENIOR in high school. She should have been
having a FABULOUS senior year, but *instead*
her mother and I were going through a **divorce**.
It was a **hurtful** time, a time I'm sure
Annie would rather *forget*.

That's why I was so EXCITED to give her
something for Christmas she *really wanted*,
a **necklace with a diamond cross** on it.

It was one of those *times* when we were shopping
and she saw **exactly** what she wanted.
Her comment went something like this:

"Wow, I would love to have that necklace,
but I know it's too much money."
The fun part for me was that I could **afford** it,
and I went back and BOUGHT it.
I *wrapped* the small box and put it in her stocking.
You know the routine, she didn't *think* she would get it.
Then on Christmas, when opening what she thinks
is just a **small** stocking gift, there it is!
The **screams** of surprise and the BIG smile
that followed was a thrill.

By February, I was living in Tempe, AZ in a condo
that was very *near* to the beauty salon
of our *good* friend, Jan McCarthy. She had cut hair
for EVERY person in our family for 17 years.

It was very late in the afternoon
when I got a FRANTIC call from Annie.
She was *talking* and *crying* at the same time.

"Dad, I lost my cross. I found the chain in my blouse,
but the cross is gone."

I tried to **calm** her. I said what *most* Dad's
should say in this kind of situation:
"I'll buy you a new one if we can't find it."
"No, Dad. I want that one!"

On to the *logical* question.
"Where do you think you might have lost it?'
"I don't know. Jan cut my hair. Maybe I lost it in her shop.
Or maybe in her parking lot. I could have lost it at Jari's,
it's the first place I drove after leaving Jan's.
It was missing when I got out of the car in her driveway."
Another sob. "I've already searched the car and Jari's driveway."

I was *willing* to go to **both** places to search for the cross.
She told me **exactly** where she had *parked* in Jan's business lot.
"I'll start with the chair in Jan's salon, and go down
the driveway to where you were parked," I told Annie.

Fortunately, Jan was **still** working,
but there was NO diamond cross in the salon.

I did run into a *friend* from our church
and she helped me *search* the parking lot.
TWICE we retraced Annie's steps, **inch by inch**
straight to her *particular* parking space.

I finally **gave up** on Jan's parking lot and jumped
in my car and to head to Annie's best friend Jari's home.
By this time it was almost *dark*. Annie and I
did another **inch by inch** search of Jari's driveway
and the car. By now it was TOTALLY dark.
We used a *flashlight*, hoping the SPARKLE of
the diamonds would **catch** our eye. That **didn't** work either.

Annie was going to a *dance* that night, so I hugged her and said,
"I'll go back to Jan's lot one more time and see if
the flashlight will catch the sparkle of the necklace there."

Again, I tried to appease Annie by promising,
"We'll either find the cross or I'll get you another one."
As before, wrong thing to say. Annie replied,
"If we don't find this one it just won't be the same."

I drove back to the now *empty* parking lot.
Before I could even get **out** of the car
I was SEIZED with an *overwhelming* impression
to **pray** about finding Annie's cross.
It was an **extremely** strange experience for me.
Something totally *out of the ordinary*, because at the same time
I found myself **arguing** with God.

I said out loud, "I'm not going to pray about finding that cross."

I *immediately* knew where that came from.
I had always **hated** it when Christians pray about
what I considered **selfish** things, like *prosperity,*
material gain and *parking places.*
And even though the cross was *special* to Annie,
it still **felt** like a *material* thing to me.

I flatly **refused** to pray and God flatly **refused**
to let me off the hook. But God kept *nudging* me,
perhaps *pushing* would be a better word.

I said again **out loud**, things like,
"I need to pray about my marriage more than a lost cross."
And, "There are children in Honduras that I care about.
They don't even have clean water to drink."
I was becoming downright **angry** with God
and I wanted God to *know* it.

I was **blatantly** ignoring all that I had ever *believed*
or *taught* about prayer. I even had the AUDACITY
to remind God that He hadn't **heard** many
of my prayers for the past four or five months.
Because if God **had**, my marriage wouldn't be *failing*.

Here I was, **losing** my life and God wanted me
to *pray* about finding a lost cross?
With that thought *stuck* in my head,
I *grabbed* the flashlight and proceeded to *search*
the parking lot for the **third** time.
This would be absolutely the FINAL time,
and I wasn't about to **ask** for God's help.

I returned to the car *empty handed*. Then an **amazing**
thing happened: Through my *anger* and *pride*
I felt God **surround** and **overwhelm** me.
I remember feeling, "OKAY, God, you win!"

Suddenly, I became *acutely* aware that there was **more**
going on than just my *praying* about finding Annie's cross.
God showed me there was a **specific**
need in my life that I must COMMIT to God.

At about 11:00 p.m., I **gave in**. I bowed my head
and said a *simple* prayer. I asked God to **help**
me find the cross, and I also COMMITTED
my *specific* need to Him. I ended the prayer by saying,
"God, I will know for sure that this
is what you want me to do if I find the cross."

I walked back for the **fourth** time, to that area
where Annie had parked. It was the **same** area
I had already searched **three** times.
There on the *asphalt*, in that same specific parking place,
was the **cross** with the diamonds *shining* up at me.

I could hardly BELIEVE my eyes.

What are the odds that God, using Annie's cross,
had broken *down* all the barriers
I had put *up* the past few months?

And what are the odds if you have **lost** your way,
God might *speak* to you to turn your life around?
Or that God will **still** love you even when you are *angry* or *doubting*?

Finally, what are the odds that if you feel
compelled to pray after reading this simple story,
God is *doing* what He has done millions of times before?

I'd say the odds are nearly 100 percent!

The Couple in Gilley's

What are the odds that something *magically*
SPIRITUAL would happen at a sports restaurant in Phoenix,
called *Gilley's,* during the final game of the *World Series* in 2005?

I *reluctantly* became a baseball fan for **two** reasons.
The first is that two of my **most** trusted friends,
Jeff Mugford and Paul Keeler, **absolutely** LOVE the sport.
They have had a **major** impact on my life when
it comes to baseball and many other things.
In my opinion, the game was *too slow* and fairly *boring*.
Besides, how can you get into a sport
that has 162 **semi-meaningless** games?
If a team wins *55* to *60 percent* of their games
they make the BIG show. It's not a *fast-action* game
like basketball and nothing like the **electricity**
of an NBA finals game in June.

But this was the way I felt about baseball,
until the *second* reason. I became a fan during the season of
2000-2001 when the *Arizona Diamondbacks* came from
nowhere to build a championship team in **less** than 4 years.
Jeff Mugford, my teammate in ministry and
tennis competitor for 25 years, introduced me
to the inside game of baseball that year.
The *Diamondbacks* clawed their way to the *World Series,*
and I was finally attending **meaningful** games in Phoenix.
A WONDERFUL man by the name of
Mike Ingram would invite me *often* as a guest
in his **tenth row, behind-the-plate**, season tickets.

WOW! I became a baseball **fanatic**
while watching Randy Johnson and Curt Schilling
pitch us to the *World Series Championship* against
the evil empire of the *New York Yankees*.
We WON in the final, at bat, in the 7th game,
by beating the *Yankee* relief pitcher Mariano Rivera -
who had **never** blown a save in his playoff history.
At the time, he was considered UNBEATABLE.
After this **unforgettable** night,
I became a baseball fan on ALL levels.

Earlier I mentioned Paul Keeler.
This is a man who **changed** my life *completely*
after a trip to Honduras together in the late 90's.
Our hearts were **broken** by the poor
and their *need* for clean water.
As a leader in our church, Paul returned
with me to *Mountain Park* to carry the message
of how ONE church could **change** the world for *hundreds*,
if not *thousands,* by bringing clean water to the villages.
The water projects and the COMMITMENT to the poor
changed our lives and the lives of countless others in our church.
Through this passion, Paul and I became friends for *life.*
Over the past 10 years, Paul has not only affected
my life *spiritually*, but he has coaxed me into becoming
a *Boston Red Sox* fan. Paul and his wife Judy are two of the most
PASSIONATE Christians I have had the privilege of knowing.
They have been there for me through *great joy* and *great sorrow.*

The fall baseball season of 2005 found me
going through a **divorce** and
recently-resigned from the church we planted in 1987,
I had lost almost EVERYTHING that mattered in my life.
One day I was wandering through my community,
driving aimlessly, when I decided to try and *medicate* my pain
by going to *Gilley's* to watch game 7 of the ALCS
(American League Championship Series).
Boston was making a **historic** comeback from a 3-0 deficit
and was now in the *game-deciding* 7th game.
Gilley's was packed with both *Yankee* and *Boston* fans.
There was NOT an open table in the place.

I stood and **watched** a couple of innings,
when a very kind young couple *invited* me to have a seat
with them and share an appetizer.
Ashamed and *depressed* about my life,
I made a *quiet* resolution to keep our conversation surface level
and not discuss ANYTHING personal.

After about 20 minutes, I got up from the table
and dialed my good friend Paul Keeler on the West Coast
to let him know I was in Phoenix watching the game.
He asked me where I was with all the background noise.
As I told him I was at *Gilley's*, Johnny Damon hit a
grand slam home run and we went CRAZY on the phone.
We ended the conversation and I sat back down with the
young couple. I was telling them about my good friend Paul,
when the young man in his late 20's got up from the table
to use the restroom. His girlfriend turned to me and asked
what I did for a living. I *scrambled* in my mind for what to say,
and ended up telling her I was a MOTIVATIONAL speaker
and did some consulting on the side.
Actually this was **partly** true, as I had just begun
to consult new church plants and was moving to
Oklahoma City in a few weeks to start CMA.

In the next few minutes, she began to **pour** her life out to me,
She was in a *4-year* relationship with this guy and they were
now living together. She was *craving* advice on whether or not
she should stay, as he was **unwilling** to COMMIT to marriage.
With much *compassion* and *understanding,* I started to give her
fatherly-advice, just like talking to my own daughters.
I explained how she should make sure he was COMMITTED
to this relationship, or YES, move out. I tried *lightly* to say,
"If he doesn't give you a ring soon, I'd be on my way out the door."

With this young woman **pouring** her heart out
so *vulnerably* in a very brief time,
the last thing I wanted was for her to **know**
I was a pastor, or that I would *judge* them
for living together. This changed, however,
when out of **nowhere**, a woman called out my name
and walked up to the table to give me a hug.
She had a baseball hat on and I *couldn't* tell who she was.

I whispered in her ear, "Who are you?"

Finally, she backed up and took off her cap, saying,
"It's Judy Keeler! After talking to you on the phone,
Paul was worried about you being here depressed by yourself,
and asked me and my sister Susan to come join you!"

What a **great surprise**. *Boston* was in the final innings,
and this young couple asked Judy and Susan
to have a seat with us. Everything was happening so *quickly*
I didn't think of asking Judy not to tell this couple
who I was or about pastoring our church the past 17 years.

Without thinking, I made my way to the restroom,
and when I returned I saw a very **shocked** look on the young
woman's face as Judy was telling her all about me
as her pastor for 10 years at *Mountain Park Community Church*.
What are the odds? My cover was **blown** and the young woman
was NOT very happy with me. I could read it all over her face,
"You set me up! Here I tell you all my dirty laundry
and you are a pastor."

I wanted to tell her I was **sorry** but Judy kept going on
and on about *Mountain Park*, how it was the *greatest*
and *safest* church she had ever been to,
and how I had made it that way. She kept saying,
"You just have to come!"

She began to brag on the interim pastor, Gerald Marvel.
I was still feeling **bad** and wanted to **apologize**,
but her boyfriend *didn't know* what we had talked about
so that would have just made everything *worse*.

Finally, to break the tension I was feeling between
me and this young woman, I said,
"I have to go, but I want you to know if you don't
have a church, Mountain Park is the safest place to go
to find out about God's love."

I told this couple about the broken side-walk out front.
We had broken up the front side walk
and placed the Bible verse that simply says,
"I have come to bind up the broken-hearted."

I looked this young woman in the eyes and said,
"I'm begging you to attend at least one time."
Then I slipped away from the table.

The game ended and *Boston* had completed a
                 4-game-in-a-row comeback to make history.
They would go on to WIN the *World Series*
        and I made the move after that to Oklahoma City.

What are the odds, after my disgraceful ending
             at *Mountain Park,* I would get a phone call in January
asking me to **come back** and **speak** one more time?
      The people there really wanted to THANK me for starting
the church and being their pastor for 17 years.
           The ending had been so *abrupt* and *painful*
      that most of the people didn't even get
                to say *goodbye* to me or my family.
I was still feeling so **much pain** that I wanted to say
           "NO" to the GRACIOUS invitation,
but Pastor Gerald convinced me I needed
          to come for *closure* and *healing* for the church
and for me and everyone else.
        I could NEVER have imagined how much
healing could take place in **one** day.

I walked into my **favorite** church of all time,
         Mountain Park, on the 3rd Sunday in January 2006.
I wondered if anyone would show because of my
      shameful ending. But to my **surprise**, the place was packed
and they gave me a standing ovation that I will NEVER forget.
      During my ministry at *Mountain Park*,
    I had told two stories, both about GRACE, over and over again.
        These stories **gripped** our lives and were somewhat
legendary to the church. One was entitled,
      "Remember the Duck" and the other was, *"Nice Pants!"*

When I walked into the church that Sunday,
        there was a **string of ducks** hanging over the doors
entering the sanctuary. It was EMOTIONAL,
        and became much more so, as Tom came out
to give announcements in **Hot Red Pants**.
      I've never hugged SO many people in all my life.
The *emotions* of that day were at a **peak**.

Between the two services I walked out into the foyer,
        surprised and *overjoyed* to find Paul and Judy Keeler,

who had just moved from Phoenix to California
but flew back for the celebration.

Judy said, "Robin you have to see something,
you're not going to believe this."

She pulled me across the foyer through hundreds of people
to the entrance doors. What are the odds, the young couple
from *Gilley's* was standing there smiling ear to ear.

Remember us?" the young woman said.
"I was so angry at you that night when I found out
you were a pastor. I had opened up my life to you
and told you I was living with this guy.
You didn't judge me, but I still felt so judged.
After you left though, Judy and I kept talking
and she insisted I come to church.
She told me about your divorce and that you were
feeling so depressed and ashamed that night
you didn't want anyone to know who you were
or how you had failed.
She convinced me this was a safe place to come
if I was hurting. Then my boyfriend came,
and now look!"
She pointed to a beautiful diamond on her hand.
"Pastor Gerald led us to Christ and now
we are getting married in a few months."

What are the odds? What are the odds God can take
ANY situation and turn it into something **good**?

What are the odds God can do something **magical** in *Gilley's*
sports bar during game 7 of the ALCS with a Pastor
who has *lost* just about EVERYTHING.
I'd say, about 100 percent.

The Blind Ethiopian Woman

T he *deal* had been made, the PROMISE given:
I would be **home** by Monday, August 7th.
I *assured* my youngest daughter, Annie,
of this when she had announced,
"We will come and stay with you two weeks if you will promise
to stay home and not work all the time while we are there."
The **"we"** included her two cousins, Whitney and Kinsey,
who were coming *with* her to Oklahoma City.

The weekend *before* they were to arrive,
I was *guest speaker* at our new church plant in Seattle.
My oldest daughter, Leah, had joined me
as *worship leader*, and she gave a mini concert.

Leah and I were having a **great** time, but on Sunday after church,
I got the *bright* idea of trying to get back
to Oklahoma City a day early. That would really **impress** Annie!

Leah drove me to the airport to see if I could
get out on **stand by**. I had a few buddy passes
with *America West* from a pilot friend
which allowed me to stand by for FIRST CLASS
at Seattle's *SeaTac* airport. I got in the first class line,
only to hear the news that **many** flights had been
backed up because of the **exceptionally** large number
of people *arriving* from the cruise ships on that Sunday.

The **friendly-sounding** name *"Krista"* was written on
the nametag of the woman working the desk,
but she wasn't *very* friendly. She told me in a *not-too-kind-voice,*

"You have no chance of getting on standby today."

I replied in as **friendly** of a voice as I could manage,
"I realize I probably won't get on a flight today,
but I'd like to stay and give it a try."

After a **wasted** hour of waiting, I GAVE UP.
I *waved* to Krista as I left the terminal, mouthing the word "thanks."
She waived back in a somewhat *friendlier* manner.
After all, she had **proven** that she was *right*,
I COULDN'T get on any flight.

Let me add here, I have **learned** over the last 10 years
that it **pays** to be kind to the people who RUN things.
And *believe* it or *not,* those people are the *ones* at the counter,
the *aisle* person at the *Phoenix Sun's* games,
the *window* person at *McDonald's,* etc…
It's **not** the *CEO's* of corporations, or the *owners* of companies.

Thanks to cell phones, Leah was *waiting* for me at the curb,
and I had managed to purchase a **positive** reservation
for a 5:40 a.m. flight on Monday.
Although I was NOT looking forward to getting up at 3:00 a.m.,
at least I'd be **sure** to make it home *on time*
and keep my PROMISE to Annie.

After all the *hassle* at the airport,
it had *still* turned out to be a very **good** day.
The Sunday morning service had been GREAT,
Leah's concert was AWESOME, we had a **great** dinner
and I had an *extra evening* with my oldest daughter.
I could STILL leave the next morning,
and be home *on time* for Annie.

That weekend I had been reading Jim Wallis' new book
"*God's Politics.*" Jim Wallis has been a **voice**
for the *poor* of the world for the past 25 years,
and I was **challenged** by a story he told about a woman
who runs a *shelter* for the homeless in Washington, D.C.
He had worked *side by side* with this woman for **25** years,
and EVERY time she got ready to serve the food,
she said the **same** simple prayer. If it hadn't been so *meaningful,*
it would have been *comical* because her words NEVER changed.

"Jesus, we know you will be coming through this breadline today,
help us to be kind to you and serve you well."

She NEVER asked anyone else to pray
and she said the SAME prayer **every day** for all
of these 25 years. She had learned well Jesus' words
in *Matthew 25* where He says, ***Whatever you have done***
for the least of these, you have done to me."
Everyday she *served* the homeless,
in her mind, she was *serving* Jesus.

That prayer had **grabbed** my heart.
I was so IMPRESSED with it, I had used it as the main
theme in my message to the newly planted *Seattle church.*
I told them, "You know our lives would be
different everyday if we saw each person as Jesus.
We would talk differently, we would listen
more intently, and we would serve people more
compassionately if we really saw them as Jesus."

So I PASSIONATELY asked that young congregation
to be the *hands* and *feet* of Jesus to the *"least of these."*
I asked them to *adopt* the simple prayer,
"Jesus we know you will be passing by our lives today,
help us to kind to you and serve you well."

For some reason that *prayer* was still on my mind
Monday morning, even though the morning
hadn't gone *very* well. I got up at 3:00 a.m.
and arrived at the car rental office only to find
it **wasn't** open for business. My heart *sank.*
What do I do NEXT? How would I **get** to the airport?
What are the odds the night worker **agreed**
to drive me to the airport at 4:00 a.m.

I walked into *SeaTac* and couldn't **believe** my eyes.
The line at the *America West* counter was at least
150 people deep, and they were all there because
of the **backup** from the day before.
At first I didn't **panic**, but as it got close to 5:00 a.m.
and I was still about **50** people back from the counter,
I knew I was in **trouble**. Then I got a BOLD idea.
The FIRST CLASS line was *empty*, and guess who was working

that counter? You guessed it, **Krista.**

As I approached her counter I asked in my **most** friendly voice, "Hey, don't they ever let the good people go home to sleep?"
She SMILED and said, "Hello, Mr. Wood." The smile seemed like a **good** sign. She did *remember* my name...
that seemed like an even BETTER sign.
It **wasn't.** As soon as she saw my ticket
was **not** first class, her *smile* turned to a *frown.*

"Mr. Wood", she said, looking me straight in the eye,
"This is not a first class ticket. You are in the wrong line."

I quickly went into my *win-her-over* mode.
I even showed her a *picture* of Annie, but NO change.
"Mr. Wood, you will have to go back to the other line."

I began to PLEAD my case about Annie and the PROMISE
I had made my daughter. If she didn't *change* her mind,
I would **miss** the flight and I would NOT get home that day.
Finally, she took my ticket and said "I will help you out today."
I don't know what brought about the *change,* but there
was **kindness** in her eyes for the first time since we met.

She was just ready to **process** my ticket,
when to my HORROR, a man pushing
a wheelchair *squeezed* past me, up to the counter.
In the wheelchair was a little elderly *woman,*
dressed in a *heavy* black robe with a black scarf over her head.

She stared *straight* ahead as the man pushing her
handed Krista a ticket. The time was **now** 5:12 a.m.
and my *anxiety* level is **rising.**
Krista turned to me and announced,
"Mr. Wood, I will help you, but you will
have to wait. She has a first class ticket."
Krista emphasized "SHE" and "FIRST CLASS."

What followed *raised* my anxiety level **another** notch.
With a *sigh,* the man reached down and *hoisted* onto the scale
one of the LARGEST suitcases I've ever seen.
How he had *managed* that suitcase while pushing
an occupied wheelchair is more than I'll **ever** figure out.

The suitcase registered **84** pounds…
34 pounds OVER acceptable weight.

Krista was unfazed "There is an $80 charge
for the overage in weight." she *calmly* informed the man.
"Ma'am, I am just the taxicab driver.
This is a blind woman from Ethiopia.
She doesn't speak English. She has no money.
Her family put her in my taxi this morning
and asked me to deliver her to America West.
I know she has no money."

I'm thinking Krista will be *moved* and just **waive**
the fee, but **no** such luck. She gets on the speakerphone
and announces, "Paging an Ethiopian interpreter,"
and then to make matters **worse**, she *leaves*
the desk and *disappears* into a room behind her.
The time is now 5:17 a.m.

What follows next could have been
hilarious if I hadn't been so **panicky.**
Krista returns with a *small* box that didn't look
much larger than a shoe box, and says,
"Let's see how much weight we can get into this box."
They unzip her suitcase and there is *nothing* in it
but *bulky, heavy* robes, the woman's native Ethiopian apparel.
I'm thinking to myself, "*They surely aren't going to try
and stuff those robes…even one robe, into that small box.*"
But that's EXACTLY what they were trying to do.

The time is now 5:20 a.m. and I'm *sweating bullets.*
I reached into my pocket, pulled out ALL the money
I had on me…four $20 bills…and say to Krista,
"Here's the deal. I'll pay for her luggage
if you process me at the same time."
I didn't offer to pay with PURE motives,
I **wanted** to get on that flight,
I **wanted** to be on time for Annie.

Obviously Krista hadn't **read** my thoughts because she said,
"Mr. Wood, this is so kind of you."

In all *honesty* to myself, I couldn't leave her thinking that.

"I'm not being kind. I want to make that flight in time
to be there for my daughter. And I mean it,
you have to process me at the same time you do her."

Krista replies, "I'll do it if you are doing the paying."
I was, and she did.

My plane wasn't taking off until 5:40 a.m.
I still had *10 minutes* to get through security.
When I rounded the corner, my heart *sank*.
There must have been **100** people
ahead of me to get through security.
I dropped my bag and simply said,
"Well God, I tried. That was my last $80, but I tried."

At that moment the **taxi driver** came around the corner
pushing the wheelchair with the blind *Ethiopian woman* in it.
He **caught** my eye as I waved and said, "Have a good day."

He walked toward me and said,
"I'm done. You, sir, are taking her to the gate."
He *placed my hands* on the wheelchair and continued,
"At least, with the wheelchair, you can get to the front of the line.
I'm out of here," and he was GONE.

With the wheelchair, we DID get through security in no time,
but then I **realized** I had to PUSH her to her gate.
I have to be TRUTHFUL, it entered my mind to just **leave** her
with security and tell them I had to **catch** my own flight.

Just as **quickly** as it came, the *selfish* thought was replaced
with the one that had been *running* through my mind earlier:
*"Jesus, we know you will be coming through SeaTac today.
Help us be kind to you and serve you well."*

It had been SO easy to **preach** about that prayer
on the previous Sunday, but when put to the test, I almost **flunked**.

I got out her ticket jacket and RUSHED to gate B3.
Arriving there, I glanced at my own ticket to see
how much *farther* I had to run.

So what are the odds my gate was **also** B3?
And what are the odds that just as we got there
an Ethiopian interpreter showed up?
We had **one minute** before the doors were to close.

The *woman* and the *interpreter* began to talk in her native language,
and he turned to me and said she wanted to **thank** me
for bringing her to the gate. She gave me a **hug**.

Although we couldn't *communicate*, we ended up sharing a seat,
until she changed planes in Phoenix.

What are the odds my **encounter** with the blind
Ethiopian woman would help me **see** Jesus?
And **keep** my promise to Annie?

What are the odds God cares about the details of our daily lives?
100 percent!

One Wedding in Oklahoma City

It was the year 2001 when I remember my friend Gary Kendall and I first began to dream about developing a church planting foundation. We had each planted successful churches, but vividly recalled the struggles and hardships of starting a new church with very few resources.

Gary and I ENVISIONED a *different* way of starting churches. We dreamed of something that could **empower** pastors to plant new churches in **every** major city of the United States. This foundation would locate cities that were *conducive* to launching a new church, assess pastors with a PASSION for planting, and finally, provide the necessary *financial aid* needed to succeed. In addition, we would *provide* training, coaching, and mentoring. The whole idea was to provide the *finances* needed to launch the new church with an *adequate* base so the pastor wouldn't have to be *bi-vocational*. It was obvious from the beginning we would need **donors** with DEEP pockets and a large number of FAITHFUL givers, to make our **dream** a **reality**.

One of the **first** things we did was approach *two* individuals who were **known** to be GENEROUS donors.

They bought into our **dreams**, and because of their
backing EMOTIONALLY, SPIRITUALLY and FINANCIALLY,
Church Multiplication Association (CMA) became a reality.

When we founded CMA, we had a *goal*
of starting **four** new churches the first year.
We would then *branch out* and hopefully
plant **eight** churches the next year, with the goal
of each church *multiplying* every **three** to **four** years.
Under this *multiplication* strategy, we felt we could
plant possibly **100** churches in ten years.
But God had *another* plan, one much BIGGER
than we had even **dared** to dream.
Over the past three years, CMA has *planted,*
restarted, or *assisted* with over **54** church plants.
If this trend *continues,* we could be looking at
over 500 churches in 10 years. What are the odds?

With the number of churches we could plant **increasing**,
however, the need for **additional** funding
also increased *rapidly.* We needed MORE donors
who **believed** in our dream and who would provide
the same EMOTIONAL, SPIRITUAL and FINANCIAL
support the *original* donors had so freely given.
As co-founders of CMA, Gary and I were responsible
for raising those *additional* funds.
When we realized how **quickly** we were growing,
we set out to do just that.

I had it in mind to approach a certain Mr. A
(A for *anonymous*) about becoming a donor to CMA.
I didn't know this man *personally,* but I had heard
good things about him, including his *generosity.*
I shared my intentions to meet with Mr. A
with a mutual close friend, but **immediately**
he threw *cold water* on the idea, saying,
"Robin you'll NEVER get close enough
to him to even ask for a donation."

What neither of us could have *foreseen* was
how God would use a "What Are The Odds" experience
to put us both at a *football* game in Norman, Oklahoma,

where sure enough I would **meet** Mr. A.
I found him *very personable* and *very kind.*
He seemed **sincerely** interested in what CMA was doing,
and he asked several *pertinent* questions regarding
our ministry of planting churches.
We talked for about **15 minutes** and I ended
the conversation by asking if I could contact him later
and set up an *appointment* for **further** discussion.

I'm a fairly **optimistic** person and usually go about
expecting God to do **great** things, but I have to say
I was **overjoyed** with my *unexpected* contact with Mr. A.
I couldn't WAIT to tell my friend about the
"what are the odds" meeting at the football game.

My friend won't mind that I mention here
that he has the *spiritual* gift of DISCOURAGEMENT.
His response to my enthusiasm was more *cold water.*
"The meeting will never happen Robin.
You'll get cancelled OVER and OVER again."

I didn't want to **believe** him; in fact,
I REFUSED to believe him.
I proceeded to *pursue* a meeting with Mr. A.
I *pursued,* and *pursued,* and *pursued,* but as I
set a meeting with him *time* and *time again,*
he **cancelled** each one.
The funny thing is he ALWAYS
had an *excellent* reason for canceling.
I knew he was an *extremely* busy man,
and I felt *strongly* the "What are the Odds" meeting"
was from God, so I ACCEPTED each
time and tried to *persevere.*

As the *months* passed and I still had **not**
been able to get a meeting with Mr. A,
however, my OPTIMISM started to *break down.*
I, too, began to have **doubts.** Maybe my friend was **right**;
maybe I was NEVER going to get close enough
to the *elusive* Mr. A to even **ask** for a donation.
I was going through some major *emotional* challenges

at this point in my personal life as I was trying
to *recuperate* from my recent divorce.
I also had some health problems going on,
so my faith was **shaken** very much
by my *own* circumstances.

During this period I was living in Oklahoma City,
I definitely **didn't** want to be there. I even *joked* about
being an EXILE in the great state of Oklahoma.
My *home* was in Phoenix, my *heart* was in Phoenix,
and I intended to return **ASAP**.
To tell you how **serious** I was about this,
I had made a COMMITMENT to myself
that I would NOT make any **new** friends.
At that time I had only **9** personal acquaintances in
Oklahoma City, and I was *determined* to keep it that way.

But God had a *different* plan in mind,
and another "What are the Odds" story
was unfolding. My close friend thought it would be
a **good** thing for me to begin *working out* again.
He arranged personal sessions for me
at his company's *Wellness Center* with John,
his own trainer. John was an **awesome** guy
and helped me put together a workout schedule.
I had **no** choice but to *accept* his friendship
and help. I didn't *realize* it at the time,
but the *walls* I'd built of NOT wanting to make
any more friends was coming **down** as John
soon became my **tenth** friend in Oklahoma City.

John and I did have ONE very common thread.
He, **too**, over the past couple of years,
had been *overcoming* the **trauma** of a divorce.
He was just *beginning* to see a young woman,
Tiffany, who he was falling in LOVE with.
In fact, as soon as I met her,
Tiffany became my **11th** friend in town.
My guard was **down** and we built a **good** friendship
in a short time. I even felt *safe* enough to tell him
about my own *divorce* as a pastor and share about
the **pain** I'd been *struggling* so much with.

Within *four* months of knowing John and Tiffany,
I was **surprised** one day when he called and
asked me to perform their **marriage** ceremony.
When he told me the date, however,
I was *immediately* tempted to turn him **down**.
I LOVE to play golf, and played on the college team
for 4 years at *Anderson University*.
John and Tiffany's wedding happened to be ON the day
of *Anderson University's Annual Alumni Golf Tournament*:
a major **highlight** in my life every year.
I had WON the event **twice** and, of course,
was hoping to **win** again. It was also an *opportunity*
to see great friends I only get to see **once** a year on that day.

Unfortunately, there comes a time in every person's life
where adult *decisions* are required,
and this was **one** of them. The alumni tournament
would have to **wait** until next year. I decided to **do**
the wedding for my two *newest* friends.
And what do you think the odds are, that at their
small backyard wedding in rural Oklahoma,
one of the 32 people present would be the **elusive** Mr. A?

Furthermore, what are the odds I would
deliver a message and Mr. A would like it so **well**
that he approached me *afterwards* to say,
"Robin, you're damn good, and I want to meet with you."

Because of the *decision* to do that wedding,
I was in Mr. A's office within a month.
The meeting with him was a *turning point*
in the CMA ministry, as he PLEDGED
to become one of our **largest** donors.
Without his help, we would NEVER be able to
accomplish the **dream** God placed in our *hearts* at CMA.

What are the odds I would know
only **10** people in Oklahoma City,
that I would be asked to do **one** wedding,
and that God would *orchestrate* the whole scenario
of events to bring about a financial *commitment*
to EMPOWER 55 church plants over the past 3 years?

What are the odds I would have **two**
random-chance meetings with one
of the most *generous* men I've ever met?
And what are the odds that all of this would lead
to a total of **25,000** people in attendance for
the **55** churches with CMA on Easter Sunday 2007?

I would say the odds are about 100 percent with God.

Two Principals in Ohio

Over the past two years
while working as a consultant with
Church Multiplication Association (CMA),
I have had the PRIVILEGE of mentoring and coaching
over **forty** church planters across the United States.
Two specific pastors had *planted* 2 new churches with many
of the necessary resources **missing**, such as money,
a *strong* leadership team, a *good* location,
necessary equipment, and *exceptional* music.
We began to discover that in **many** of our new church plants,
all of these *key* factors were **missing**.

This is a story of *two* churches and
the MIRACLE that brought about their success.
Both churches had **one** significant need
in common: a good **location**, attractive
and large enough to seat over 200 people.
Both churches were considered *re-launches*
with CMA and located in Ohio.
The pastors are Tom Plank in Cincinnati,
and Kevin Schweiger in Lebanon,
two cities about 30 miles apart.
Both of the churches had, at one time,
enjoyed a good start, but were *struggling* because neither
had been able to get into *well-located* schools.
Tom was running about **60** in attendance
after 10 years, and after two years,
Kevin was meeting with about **10** people in his home.

Without a church building, the safest,
most *visible* and *affordable* place to meet
is in a local school. A high school *auditorium*, or a
cafetorium of a middle or elementary school is best.
But finding schools **willing** to rent their facilities
long-term are *difficult*, and often times, *impossible* to find.
It's hard to gain the TRUST of principals who **don't** know
the church leadership, and for **good** reason.
Both *principals* and *teachers* are impacted negatively
if ALL terms of the contract are **not** met,
or if the classrooms are **not** well-maintained.
Teachers have NO patience for those
who disrupt their classroom.

So Tom, Kevin, and myself, decided to
partner together for *training, strategy,* and *coaching.*
Both pastors agreed the *location* was their
biggest obstacle, and both were *emphatic* that
the best school locations were absolutely **closed** to them.
As their coach, I just couldn't *accept* the fact that
the local schools were closed to these two church plants.
I'm not completely **obstinate**, though my friends might say
I'm very *close.* I just can't seem to take "NO" for an answer.

I was meeting with Tom in Cincinnati one day,
when I asked him, "Tom, where is the nearest
high school from here?" Almost before he could reply,
I was heading out the door to my car.
He had NO choice but to **follow** me.

"You're not just going to barge in
and ask for an appointment, are you?" he pleaded.
"You've got it. That's exactly what we're going to do.
We need God's favor and if I understand scripture correctly,
it says, 'Ask and you will receive. Seek and you will find.
Knock and the door will be opened to you.'"

Tom reminded me that he had been
turned down many times for this very school.
I won't go into the details, but the results were **awesome**.
We walked in, met the principal, and by that afternoon,
we were **signing** contracts for this outstanding
location at *East Lacota High School* in Cincinnati.

Two weeks later I found myself in Lebanon, Ohio
with Kevin, doing the **same** thing I had done with Tom.
I practically **forced** Kevin out the door
and into my car. As we drove to the nearest school,
I gave him the **same** speech I had given to Tom.
Once again, Kevin *reminded* me that he
had been **turned down** when he asked
to use this particular Elementary School.

So, what are the odds for the second time,
we would walk into a BEAUTIFUL school
and meet with the principal **without** an appointment?
You've got it. With God's favor,
we got an appointment with the principal.
Kevin and I began a conversation as to **why**
we were there, and the principal gave
her position as to **why** they were reluctant
to rent their school to a church.

But suddenly she looked at me
as if she just had a new thought.
"Are you a national consultant
with a national foundation?" she asked.

"Yes," I answered. I often *introduce* myself to principals
with the credentials of CMA, hoping to gain some **credibility**.
Then they can go online and see our *National Organization*
and our *desire* to plant churches all across the United States.
However, I had **not** introduced myself to this particular
principal this way, so her question **surprised** me.

"My husband is the principal of East Lacota High
in Cincinnati. I think he met you last week."
"That's me," I said, amazed at how this was going.

For the first time, she looked straight into
my face and smiled. "My husband liked you.
I'm going to sign a contract with you also."

WOW! What are the odds?
We approached only ONE school in a city
as large as Cincinnati, and got a **contract** with
a principal where we had been *turned down* before.

What are the odds I am meeting a principal **30 miles** away,
who happens to be his *spouse*? God is **awesome**!

On the following Christmas Eve, both churches opened
their doors to worship in their new school facilities.
Pastor Tom's church, *Journey Church*, had
206 in attendance, and Pastor Kevin's church,
Turtle Creek, had **88** in attendance. What are the odds?

When God is involved, about 100 percent!

The Flood

After 21 days of being on the road consulting with several of our CMA churches across the country, I was **more** than ready to come home and get some *rest* for a few days. I pulled into my driveway and waved *'hello'* to Katherine, an elderly woman who lives across the street in my *adult* community in Sarasota. Seeing Katherine took me *back* in thought to the week before, when I had asked my assistant, Patsy, to *pray* for me in a specific way. Since moving into this community earlier that year, I had realized I did **not** know any of my *neighbors* except Katherine, a nice Christian lady who would say "Hi" to me when I returned from my travels every 2-3 weeks. I had asked Patsy to *pray* I would develop some close FRIENDSHIPS so I could *share* God's love. It had been *over* a year since I had led someone to Christ personally. It was a very **small** request; I simply felt the **loss** of my *passion* toward people living **without** God's love.

I got my suitcase out of the car and breathed a *sigh of relief* as I walked into to my condo. I *instantly* realized, however, that something didn't *smell* right. Actually, something didn't *sound* or *feel* right underneath my feet either.

I looked around and could NOT believe what I saw:
my 2,000 square foot space was holding **6 inches** of water.
The room *smelled* and *felt* like a musty sauna.
I recalled having turned the air *up*
to **85 degrees** before I left.

"Slush, slush, slush" was all I heard ringing through
my head as **exploding** feelings of *anger, frustration,*
and *confusion* set in. I walked from room to room
totally **overwhelmed** by my *surreal* circumstances.
I was *paralyzed* and *frantic* inside.
What in the world had happened?
My first *thought* was there must have been
an outdoor *sprinkler* that **broke**, or
the person above me had a *water leak.*
Where was this large amount of water **coming** from?

After a number of *unsuccessful* calls
trying to reach the *condo association director,*
I opened up the yellow pages and dialed
the first number I found for water removal.
I'll **never** forget the catch phrase,
"Call George the Mold Master!"
That's **exactly** what I did, and soon George was on his way.

George arrived, a *jolly* man in his late 50's who
was very **serious** about the business of **conquering** mold.
After seriously *combing* my house with his high-tech
water detector, he was **convinced** the water line
to the refrigerator was the *culprit.*

George looked at me and said, "This is good news Robin!
It's only the water line, and I think we've caught it in time!"

How could this be **good** news? As he turned off
the line under the sink, he explained if we went
to work *right away* there might **not** be a problem
with mold because it was *clean* water from the ice-maker.
We didn't know **how long** the water
had been standing there, but he seemed
pretty *convinced* it wasn't a **huge** problem.
George was ABSOLUTELY committed to **stop**
any mold from taking root in my home.

Over the next *few* hours, he was on a **mold-mission**
alright. He set up all of his *"exclusively-newest"*
equipment that was going to *suck* the water out.
He brought in his young partner and about
20 other fans and dehumidifiers.
Then he looked at me with a *crazed* look in his eyes,
pressed START, and said, "Follow me."

I followed him from *room to room* as he kept
showing me with his water detector tool
how water was being *soaked up*
by the walls, repeating **emphatically**,
"We have to stop it here. We have to stop it here..."

Then he said with serious concern and conviction
in his voice, "Robin, I have to tear off all the baseboards
to keep mold from forming and growing
in every room, then taking over the condo."

He was so **intense** that I just said,
"Do whatever you have to do George."
I felt *defeated*, wondering **why** and **how** this
could be *happening* to me.

I was leaving on **another** 6-day trip
the next day, so I let George *loose* on his mission
in my house *without* many more questions.
In RETROSPECT, I wish I would have taken
some time to think through my options,
but *George the Mold Master* was on a roll with his
big machines and baseboards already flying.
His wife and some *more* people from his
"mold team" showed up to put my furniture
on *Styrofoam* before finishing up for the day.

I woke up the next morning after a *sleepless* night
with **loud** fans and de-humidifiers.
George arrived again, ready to **fight** the mold.

"George," I said, "How much is this all going to be?"
He answered me immediately,
"Don't worry, your insurance will cover it."

That's when a very **sick** feeling hit me.

I wasn't sure I had *insurance* for this.

When I had bought the place, there was insurance
included in the *association fees* that covered
the *outside* and *structural* part of the property.

In my opinion at the time, I didn't have **anything**
to **protect** on the inside, so I didn't **buy** renter's insurance.

I said, "George, I don't think I have insurance
because I put 20 percent down and I wasn't
required to buy insurance for the building.
So how much do you think this is going to cost?"

"Oh, just about $2,000 or so." he answered.

I left the next day and when I *returned* the following week,
George had kept at least **one** promise.

Everything was *dry* and the condo *smelled* okay.
However, the baseboards were still *torn off* the walls
and *scattered* everywhere. The furniture was all over,
and the place was overall a big WRECK.

George came by to get his check and I asked him
nervously, "So when do you come and put the place
back together, and the baseboards back on?"

He looked at me with a level *gaze* and said,
"Oh I don't do that, I just do everything to remove
the water and make sure there is no mold in your walls."

"You don't do that'?" I exclaimed. "Who does?
You will have to find someone to finish this up."
I couldn't believe what I was hearing.
My little condo looked worse now
than it did with all the water in it!"

If I wasn't feeling sick *enough* already
about this, what came next did me **in.**
"How much did you say you need, George?"

Had I heard him correctly? He repeated, "$6,000."
I didn't know **what** to say.

I had *never* anticipated paying for a flood **without** insurance.

He said, "You can pay me in installments if you'd like."

My head was *swimming* as I wrote him the first check.
George the *Mold Master* said thanks, and left.

On a *conference call* later that afternoon with my staff,
I shared my **frustration** and feelings of being **overwhelmed.**
Here we were, in *full gear* preparing for our
.   *4th Annual CMA Church Planters Conference,*
our **biggest** event of the year was just
two weeks away and my *home* was a **disaster**.
To say the least, my spirits were **down**.
Gary Kendall told me he was *praying* for me
with the whole situation. He knew I **didn't**
have insurance and had asked me
if I was going to be **able** to pay the *$6,000*.
I told him that George the *Mold Master* gave
a **good** report on the mold and a **payment** plan I could do.

I *thanked* Gary for his concern and then
I will **never** forget what I said next.
"Gary, you know what I hate about the $6,000
and the flood, is that there's just no good story tied to it!"

Gary quickly responded,
"Oh, I'm sure you will come up with something!"

We all *laughed* on the phone together,
as my staff all knows I've been writing
these crazy "what are the odds" stories.
But there wasn't a **good** story tied to my *flooded* condo.
In my mind, I was out *$6,000*, and all for **nothing**.
And my place was still TOTALLY unlivable.

I decided to *drive* up to the corner of my neighborhood
and get some *sushi*. I remember thinking SARCASTICALLY,
"If I eat some raw fish maybe I'll die. I have great life insurance."
Hope you're *smiling.*
I walked into this new sushi place and
was sitting down when I *noticed* four young men
eating at the table next to mine.
They were in their twenties, and it looked
like they had just *ended* their work day.

I was feeling **overwhelmed** so I said a short prayer.
"God, what am I going to do about my condo?"

The next thing I knew, I felt God **urging** me
to go over to the table of young men and *ask*
if they knew of anyone who did *baseboards*.
I've had **many** encounters with God, but this one
takes the cake. It became a HEAVINESS in my chest
and I just knew God was *asking* me to go
talk to them about it. The thing is,
I really **didn't** want to talk about the frustrating situation,
I wanted to be *defeated* by it for a while and just **give up**.
The baseboards could just *stay* all over the house.
I didn't care. I *argued* with God inside,
but the *feeling* to get up just got **stronger**.
So, what are the odds, I got up and walked over
to tell my story about *"the flood"* and inquire
if they knew of *anyone* who could help me.

I explained I was *new* to the area and
told them about George the *Mold Master*.
They laughed as I described George and his **mold-madness**,
and then I told them about the *remaining* baseboard problem.

What are the odds, one of the young men
sitting at the table said, "Hey that's what my boss does.
I mean, he does remodel jobs, but he can help you
get those baseboards back on. In fact,
I will make a call right now and have him call you."

He took my cell number and *before* I went to bed that night,
his boss, Matthew had *called* and *scheduled* a time
the next day to *come out* and *give* me a bid.

After *seeing* the condo, he said one of his guys
named John could *definitely* get it done for me.
I asked, "How much? I'm already into this $6,000."

He replied, "Well you've got two options. If I bid it,
you are looking at about $2,000 more.
But if you hire another guy who works for me, John,
he can save you quite a bit."

I asked, "Can he keep me under $1,000?"

"Yes he can," Matthew replied.

So we called John to come for the job, and this is
where the **real** "What are the Odds" story begins.

John came to work on the baseboards over the next two days.
He seemed to be doing a **fantastic** job throughout the condo.
He used as many broken baseboards as *possible*
to **save** me money. We didn't talk much at all
because I was on the phone staying *engulfed* in
CMA business. When I'm at home in Florida,
I usually spend **most** of my days there catching up
on *coaching* about 35 pastors in church plants
and *returning* all my messages.
Over the two days John was in my house
I had **two** major *conference calls* with all our
CMA pastors and staff members, and was **consumed**
with *finalizing* the last minute details for our
national conference the following week in Kansas City,
our **biggest** event of the year.
I stayed on the phone *non-stop* as John worked away.

It wasn't until the *second* day that we actually
connected and had a longer conversation.
I asked John if he'd like something to drink.
He accepted, then smiled at me curiously and said,
"Robin, what do you do for a living and what's up
with all those phrases you use about churches?"

I started *laughing*, and realized for the first time
how **funny** it must be to *overhear* me
working away on the phone for two days straight.
I guess I'm not *in touch* at all with how **loud**
I am on the phone or how much I **pace**
back and *forth* through different rooms *exclaiming*
all my PHRASES into the phone like,
"It's Not That We Are Just Planting Churches,
It's the Kind of Churches We Are Planting....
Everybody's Got Something Big Going On....
You Never Know Who Is Going To Be

Faithful At Your Church...."
and there are many more I'm sure.

I began to tell him about CMA and how our
organization **starts** new churches all across the country.
After a *brief* explanation, John looked at me,
pointing his finger, and said,
"I will never go back to church again."
He continued with one of the most **hurtful** stories
about his *experience* in the church I have heard in a **long** time.

I dropped my head and replied,
"I know John, that's why we are planting
the kind of churches we are planting.
So many people have been hurt by churches."

"Well, I'm done with church," John said.
I nodded. "Yeah, I get it."

But I can never **stop** there. I looked at John and simply said,
"If you went to one of our churches, you would be
fully accepted and you wouldn't be turned off."

I told him about the church I had *planted*
in Phoenix and the story of the *broken* sidewalk
out front leading up to the front doors.
"We were committed to broken people. And John,
I really do get it. I don't like most churches either."

John walked outside to take some final tools
and equipment to his truck. When he came back in,
he had the bill, only *six hundred dollars*.
WOW, I was **amazed**.

"You've got to be kidding me," I said, before trying
several times to give him a tip. He *refused* to take it.

John and I talked some more. I told him I loved tennis
and what are the odds, he had just **started** playing tennis.
I said I'd love to *teach* him how to play
using *top-spin*. Then we talked a little longer.
I told him about my *divorce* and he told me about his *divorce*.
He walked out to the car one more time with two buckets
of dry wall and came back in to check each room.

He had to put some new dry wall in one closet and told me he would have to come back next time I was in town.

I was **shocked** what he said next. "Is there a church, like the ones you described here in Sarasota?"

"Yes, there is!" I exclaimed. "Well," said John, "When you come back in town, Robin,

I'll go to church with you if you take me."

What are the odds? How could everything change so quickly? "I'll do that John."

Then he stopped at the door one more time and said,

"Will you laugh with me about something?

When I get home today, I'm going to call

my sister and tell her about meeting a pastor

who starts churches all over the country,

and that I'm going to church with you.

And you know what she is going to say?

In her most sarcastically-spiritual voice, she'll say, 'John I've been praying for you, for 14 years!'"

I started to laugh. "So what will you say back John?"

"That's why I haven't gone to church!" He said.

We both couldn't **stop** laughing.

What are the odds John would say he would *actually* GO to church with me? Well, this is just the **beginning** of the story with John, me and God.

The next day, I left for a 3 week trip of *coaching* pastors in Indiana, Phoenix, and finally in Kansas City for the *CMA Conference*.

I landed in Indiana on Saturday night and was in the car traveling between churches on Sunday morning.

I was making the drive from the service at the first church I consulted with at 9 a.m., to the second church that begins at 10:37 a.m.

I turned on my radio, and what are the odds that some *"church person"* had rented the car before me and it was on a CHRISTIAN radio station!

Please don't judge me, but I just **don't** listen to CHRISTIAN radio or watch CHRISTIAN television unless I want to go to **sleep** at night.

I'm feeling the personal *judgment* even as I type.

What are the odds, I got *"Pastor Smiley"* on the radio.

You know **wh**o I'm talking about, and I like him.

Joel Osteen. I began to say out loud,

"This is a pastor who could afford a flood
in his condo and probably keep smiling."

Well, Joel then told a *personal* story of
simply *responding* to a lady at a cash register

who was really *cranky* to everyone in the line.

When it was his turn to pay for his lunch,

Joel said, "Seems like you are having a
rough day. I'm a pastor, and I just want you to know

that I care, and God cares about you
and what you are going through."

The woman started to *cry*. Joel asked her,

"What is going on in your life." She responded,
"I'm going through a divorce and losing my kids."

Joel asked her if he could say a short *prayer* for her.

You can see him *doing* it can't you?

He had just offered an act of KINDNESS. Simple story.

I begin to cry *uncontrollably* in the car after hearing this story.

I can't explain it, but I was crying so *uncontrollably*
that I had to pull the car over before I could

pull myself back together. I asked God,

"What is happening to me? What is this all about?"

I have never heard the **audible** voice of God;
however, I do know I've had a couple of *moments*

where what God was saying to me was SO clear
I just **got** it. Here are the words that will **forever**

stick in my mind that I *heard* from God
on the side of the road that day: "

Not a good story? Is $6,000 too much for John's soul?"

What are the odds, God was going to *change* John's life,
through my *flood disaster* and *$6,000*?

I then felt God ask me to *call* John

and make sure we stayed *connected* even **before**
I got back home in three weeks.

I then began to *share* that experience with **every** church
I spoke to over the next couple of weeks, and my staff.
I called Patsy and told her. At our *CMA Conference*,
I spoke on this story and what God had said to me,
"*Is $6,000 too much for John's soul?*"

In the following weeks, I was **certain**
God was going to do something BIG with this story,
but I was having trouble *getting in touch* with John.
I found out he was *slammed* with another job.
Finally Matthew had to send a *different* worker out.
I thought to myself, "*There you go again Robin,
projecting how God will work before it happens.
Did you really hear those words in your spirit?
Is $6,000 too much for John's soul?*"

Well today, as I sat down to finish this story,
I found out the *answer* to all those doubts.
I had left a number of *messages* for John telling him
I had something to tell him, and today he called me back.
When I answered the phone, he **jumped** right in saying,
"You won't believe what has happened to me
since I met you and promised to go to church with you!
I called my sister that day and we have been talking.
I got your messages about 'God doing something
big in your life concerning me.'"

What are the odds, the **next** words out of John's mouth
on the phone, were, "ROBIN, WOULD YOU BAPTIZE ME?"

I was **baffled**, almost *speechless*.
I couldn't **believe** what I was hearing. "What did you say?"

He almost shouted, "WILL YOU BAPTIZE ME?"

Then I started to tell John what had happened to me
in the car on that Sunday, the story pouring out of me.
"John, can I tell you what God said to me in my spirit?"
He quietly replied, "Yes, please do."

I told him about the radio story and how I heard

God saying to me, "Is $6,000 too much for John's soul?"

Next I asked John,
"Wait, when did you begin to open your heart to Christ?"

His response was, "That very day!"

WOW. What are the odds?

I honestly said to Gary Kendall,
"There just isn't a good story with this flood!"
I remember **shouting** those words so *vividly*.

What are the odds that NO painful experience
comes our way, that God **can't** use?
I have a friend who **always** says in *painful* circumstances,
"Well, let's don't waste the pain, let's see what God is doing."

What are the odds, God would use a condo *flood*
and a mere *$6,000* to bring one of his CHILDREN back home?

I'd say, about 100 percent John!